THE
GOLDFISH
CLUB

THE
GOLDFISH
CLUB

DANNY DANZIGER

SPHERE

First published in Great Britain in 2012 by Sphere

A CIP catalogue record for this book
is available from the British Library.

Picture credits: page 49 and 56 Sipa Press/Rex Features; page 189 Mirrorpix.

Hardback ISBN 978-1-84744-467-7
C format ISBN 978-1-84744-468-4

Typeset in Bembo by M Rules
Printed and bound in Great Britain by
Clays Ltd, St Ives plc

Papers used by Sphere are from well-managed forests
and other responsible sources.

MIX
Paper from
responsible sources
FSC
www.fsc.org   FSC® C104740

Sphere
An imprint of
Little, Brown Book Group
100 Victoria Embankment
London EC4Y 0DY

An Hachette UK Company
www.hachette.co.uk

v.littlebrown.co.uk

For those who didn't make it . . .

High Flight

Oh! I have slipped the surly bonds of Earth
And danced the skies on laughter-silvered wings;
Sunward I've climbed, and joined the tumbling mirth
Of sun-split clouds – and done a hundred things
You have not dreamed of – wheeled and soared and swung
High in the sunlit silence. Hov'ring there,
I've chased the shouting wind along, and flung
My eager craft through footless halls of air . . .

Up, up the long, delirious burning blue
I've topped the wind-swept heights with easy grace
Where never lark, or ever eagle flew –
And, while with silent, lifting mind I've trod
The high untrespassed sanctity of space,
Put out my hand, and touched the face of God.

John Gillespie Magee, Jr
1922–1941

CONTENTS

CONTENTS

INTRODUCTION

In 1923, Frederick Stanley Mockford was a senior radio officer at Croydon Aerodrome on the outskirts of south London, then the busiest and most prestigious airport in the country. It was also the first airport in the world to introduce air traffic control. Mr Mockford was asked to come up with a word that could be used to indicate an aviation emergency situation, easily understood by ground staff and aircrew alike, no matter what their native language.

As most of the traffic he dealt with came from Le Bourget Airport in Paris, Mockford suggested the word 'Mayday' from the French *m'aider*, which means 'help me', and he advised repeating it three times. Mayday. Mayday. Mayday. This word was only to be used for a vessel – for almost immediately his system was adopted by ships as well – in the 'most grave and imminent danger', in which loss of life was a strong possibility.

For less serious situations, dangerous but perhaps not mortally so, he came up with the distress call Pan Pan, Pan, from the French word *panne*, meaning 'breakdown', and *Sécurité, Sécurité, Sécurité*, for the lowest level of danger, *sécurité* meaning 'safety'.

There are several different types of emergency landings for aircraft, whether planned or unplanned: a forced landing, a precautionary landing, a crash landing, or a ditching, which is a crash landing on water. Unfortunately, the last two categories are nearly always a Mayday situation.

Almost exactly ninety years before Mr Mockford invented the distress call system, Peter Brusey Cow opened a shop, P. B. Cow & Co., in Bishopsgate, London, selling lace and linen. The firm diversified and prospered; in fact, in 1851 it was the first company to introduce waterproof tweed commercially, and won an award at the Great Exhibition at Crystal Palace. As time went on, the firm continued to diversify, this time into rubber manufacture, and it made diving suits and hot water bottles – something of a speciality – sink plugs, toys, rubber bungs and, in the 1930s, registered Li-Lo, an inflatable air bed.

By the time the Second World War broke out, P. B. Cow & Co. was one of the world's largest manufacturers of air-sea rescue equipment, including life jackets – promptly nicknamed Mae Wests by American servicemen in honour of the pneumatic American actress – and inflatable dinghies, which were carried in nearly all British fighter aircraft, including the Spitfire and the Hurricane.

Mr C. A. 'Robbie' Robertson was the chief draughtsman at P. B. Cow, and, as a representative of one of the largest producers of sea and air rescue equipment, also responsible for liaising with the Ministry of Aircraft Production, which had been set up by Winston Churchill when he became Prime Minister in the early summer of 1940. Incidentally, the man put in charge of the Ministry, who pursued his task with energetic, almost demonic zeal, was the press baron Lord Beaverbrook.

Aeroplanes were by now regularly being shot down, and surviving aircrew would often feel they owed their survival in part to the life jackets and dinghies made by P. B. Cow & Co., and were drawn to visit the company and discuss their ditching. Aircrew would meet at the offices, and, whether pilots or gunners, navigators or bombardiers, they would exchange stories of near misses and derring-do. Having witnessed the instant comradeship that existed between those who had shared similar mortal dangers, 'Robbie' Robertson suggested these survivors start a club. Moreover, Robbie took it upon himself to start up and personally bankroll this club, to be called the Goldfish Club: gold to represent the value of life, and fish, well, all too obviously to symbolise the watery landings. The Armed Forces put up no objections, although the Royal Navy insisted the club badge, a white-winged goldfish flying over two blue waves, be sewn on to the Mae Wests, and the RAF regulated that it be located under the left-hand battle-dress pocket.

News of the formation of the club spread rapidly, even to prisoner-of-war camps, and by the end of the war the Goldfish Club was nine-thousand strong. When Robbie left P. B. Cow in 1947 to start another company, he retained all the club records and continued the administration and running of the club at his own expense. In the summer of 1951, he organised a reunion dinner at the White House restaurant in London's Mayfair, and a couple of years later it was decided to keep the club going on a permanent basis, managed by a committee of members, i.e. those who had ditched their aircraft, something Robbie had never personally experienced.

And so it is, seventy years since the first informal meeting of the Goldfish Club in 1942, that five hundred members, paying an annual subscription fee of five pounds, continue to meet once a year for an annual dinner, and receive a quarterly newsletter full of good-natured jokes and cartoons, news of new members and obituaries of departed friends.

DAVID LEATHER

We're going to be damn lucky if we come through this night . . .

The group of Tent No. 69 at PG 73. David Leather is third on the right, with shorn hair. Cecil Langton is second on the left.

War was declared in September 1939 and I decided before Christmas of that year that I had to get involved. I didn't want to join the Army; I was brought up at a time when there were still lots of wounded soldiers from the First World War all over the place, terrible sights of wounded soldiers with amputations, these poor men who had been gassed and shell-shocked. So I volunteered for the RAF.

We were forming a new squadron, and our planes were the Blenheim Mk V, called a Bisley. It was a safe, steady, reliable plane; you never had any qualms about it coming to a crash. They were powerful enough, 180 miles an hour, and they could climb to ten thousand feet, which was the max, because you had no oxygen above that. The only bad thing about the Bisley was that they had put in a lot of extra weight when they improved it, but kept the same engine, so they had a reputation for being a bit underpowered.

There were three people in each plane. I was the navigator. My crew consisted of the wireless operator/air gunner, a nice lad called Graham Wicks. We enjoyed each other's company, and, when off duty, he and I would get out on our bicycles and visit churches; he would play the organ while I'd wander around the churchyard. The pilot was a Canadian called Cecil Langton, who came from Vancouver; he was younger than Graham and me by several months, so we called him Junior.

Our first operational sortie was to fly to Burma. There were thirty planes going out. The first leg of the trip was from Redruth in Cornwall to Gibraltar. I remember leaving early on a lovely sunny summer's day in June 1942, and as we passed over the Scilly Isles I thought that could be the last time I would see the United Kingdom. I knew it was a distinct possibility I'd have a short life, although that didn't worry you at that age.

Redruth to Gibraltar was achieved with no problems; my navigation was perfect. We spent two days in Gibraltar, and although

Graham and Junior couldn't swim, all three of us went for a dip. But it was a very cold sea, and we were glad to get out.

We left Gibraltar on the 20th, and arrived in Malta early evening and were whipped straight out of our plane and sent down into a subterranean cave to get some sleep; these caves were basically big bomb shelters because Malta had been nearly bombed out of existence.

We took off very early the next day, about five o'clock in the morning. There were three planes in the formation, and we were the lead plane, flying at a low altitude over the sea, between three hundred and four hundred feet, to avoid the German radar on the island of Crete. I remember thinking the engine didn't sound quite right, and I made some remark to Cecil: 'Shall we turn back?' 'No,' he said, 'we'll push on.'

I've not a clue why we went in, the whole thing is a mystery. The next thing I remember was that I had my head on the navigation table and realised I had been knocked out. What's going on . . . ?! Then I realised, Wait a minute, I'm wet . . . and saw that we were in the sea: 7.26 a.m. is when we hit – at least that's when my watch stopped, so it's a fairly safe assumption that my watch stopped when we hit the water. The last record I made in my logbook was that we were ninety-eight miles north-east of Derna, Libya, on the North African coast.

Other than engine failure or fuel failure, the only other explanation is that because the pilot was flying so low, he got a bit bemused, because it's not easy to fly at that level, and we had cartwheeled into the water.

Many years after the war, the pilot of another plane from that formation – the only crew out of all the thirty planes who got back fully intact – phoned me from his home, and said, 'You hit the water three times before you finally went in.' But I haven't any recollections at all; it's like a complete wipe-out on a computer's software, and, as much as I try to get a flashback, it's gone.

At first I couldn't see Graham or Cecil, and I was worried about them, because, as I've said, neither of them could swim. 'Cecil, Graham, where are you?' I shouted out. Finally, Cecil answered, 'I'm here, David.' Cecil was lucky: one of the single-pilot dinghies had come out of the plane and he was in it. 'Where's Graham?' We looked around and he was clinging on to an auxiliary petrol tank that had broken adrift, so I swam over to him and pushed the thing towards the dinghy. Graham clambered in and then I got in too, and we three sat there.

The sun had come up, and the sea was pretty calm, and Junior said, 'Shall we try to paddle?' Well, I used to sail a lot, and I knew paddling ninety-eight miles was not on. 'No, forget it,' I said. And so we just sat through the day. The sun was beating down, and we got very sunburned. I remember we saw a few flying fish go by, and we heard two planes in the distance, but they could have been anything, German, Italian or RAF.

We didn't know at the time what a terrible state Graham was in, but as the gunner he had the mounted guns between his legs, and as we had fallen out of the sky they had ripped him right the way down his thighs. There was no sign that Graham was bleeding to death, but that was surely what was happening.

At the early stages Graham was as alert as we were, but later on he was obviously fading away. And then he began falling into the water, so we found a bit of cord and tied that round his wrists to hold him into the dinghy. He didn't say a word until about midday, when he suddenly piped up, 'Don't panic, boys, we'll be picked up at eight tonight.'

We thought the other planes would have alerted Alexandria we had gone down, and someone would attempt an air-sea rescue, but it was the wrong day for that, we learned later. It was 21 June 1942, which was the day Rommel's Panzerarmee Afrika captured Tobruk. Allied forces were overrun and twenty-five thousand British and Commonwealth troops were taken prisoner by the Germans, so the coast would have been in chaos and an air-sea rescue out of the question. But we didn't know that, and, as the day wore on, one began to think, Are we going to get out of this? Is someone going to pick us up? The sun was now going down, and the sea getting up a bit, and it was becoming very cold, and I certainly thought to myself, We're going to be damn lucky if we come through this night . . .

But, lo and behold, at 8.05 p.m., I saw this speck in the distance and realised it was a ship. As it gradually got closer, we saw that it wasn't a British ship; it was in fact an Italian aircraft carrier, called the SS *Aquila*, which was being used by the Italians as a hospital ship. We began screaming and shouting and waving as much as we could: 'Over here! We're here!' And, finally, this enormous thing came alongside, and a lifeboat was lowered, and they dumped us pretty unceremoniously into the bottom of that.

Graham must have died just before, or very shortly after, we were rescued. There was some discussion going on in Italian about what to do with Graham, which we didn't understand, between the sailors in the lifeboat and the crew in the boat above us, and the next thing that happened was that Graham was unceremoniously taken out of the dinghy and just dumped in the sea, still with his inflated Mae West on. My last sight of Graham was him bobbing away with his head back, and that was the end of him, no burial or anything.

They piggybacked us up the rope ladders and dropped us on the deck, and then we were just ignored, although I was in quite a lot of pain as I had got badly bruised and contused when we crashed. But even though it was a hospital ship, there was no examination for wounds, or anything.

We were interrogated for a very short time, but not brutally, and we didn't have much information to give anyway. And then we were forgotten about. The *Aquila* had been picking up German wounded to return to Benghazi and Derna, and was full of Afrika Korps, young men like ourselves, but Germans, who more or less ignored us, which was understandable.

After a couple of days we docked at Naples, I was put on a stretcher and left on the dock in the sun. I remember I could see Mount Vesuvius. By this time I was suffering, and I thought, Well, this surely is it . . .

Eventually I was put into an ambulance and taken to a place called Caserta, which was an enormous hospital that had been used for the Italo-Ethiopian war. It was run by the Sisters of Mercy, who hadn't much mercy; they were pretty callous, really, and ignored us. But I suppose we were lucky in that it was a hospital, so at least we had beds, although you had to learn how to live with bed bugs, which dropped everywhere, and dysentery, which was prevalent. I got dysentery in that ward, which was not nice.

One of the particularly memorable fellows in my ward, which was a big, long room with around forty people, was a little Arab farmer with his brain hanging out of his head. This poor chap had been riding across the desert on his donkey, minding his own business, and, like with the Taliban today, he had gone over an IED [improvised explosive device], and got blown up and lost both his legs. We were boys going out on that Blenheim flight, but I stopped being a boy when I saw that little Arab man with his legs blown off.

I was on a diet of Italian *grissini* breadsticks; I got two of those a day, and a pint of water, which might occasionally have a bit of rice in it, and that was it. This went on for a long time, and I needed food. On my twenty-first birthday, which was 5 August 1942, I received a cigarette parcel from some friends in Canada. I didn't smoke anyway, but we all recognised that cigarettes were currency during the war, and I managed to persuade an Italian guard to bring in some peaches in exchange for my cigarettes. I already had a Red Cross tin of rice I'd been saving, and so I had peaches and rice for my twenty-first birthday party. I'll never forget that meal.

Eventually, they decided to evacuate that hospital and moved us all on a hospital train to Castel San Pietro, south of Bologna, a very nice train, very comfortable, clean white sheets, no bed bugs. This hospital was again run by nuns, but this time we were well looked after. But eventually they thought we were fit enough to go into a prisoner-of-war camp, and we were moved there by train, about twenty of us, and there was a very nice Italian officer, called Captain Bucci, a gentleman, who treated us like human beings. This time there was no shouting or screaming, or treating us as enemy. We were in Italian uniforms because we had nothing else to put on, and these puttee things that we wrapped around our feet. We stopped at one station after another, and I sometimes look back and wonder why we didn't try to escape, although I suppose we weren't in a physical state to walk far. And then we arrived at Prigione di Guerra 73, PG 73, where we stayed for nearly three years.

What do you do as a prisoner of war for three years? There were musical instruments, and we had a very good brass band, which could play all types of music. I learned to play bridge, and also some people put on these radio-type plays, which were very good, and that was a relaxation from the sheer monotony of doing bugger all. But I wonder how we survived. There were no books, no facilities for writing.

I had various muckers in that camp, like George Chitty, a nice young boy who in his civilian life was a junior in a Sainsbury's store in Chertsey. Another friend was George Darville, who'd been the rear-gun operator in a Lancaster, and had got out by parachute. I said, 'After the war we should keep in touch,' and he said, 'No, no, it won't work, we're from completely different backgrounds.' His father worked at the docks in east London, and I went to public school, you see.

I missed England, and frequently thought of my home in Yorkshire. I think if you've lived in the Dales for eighteen years of your life it's imprinted on your mind for ever, and conjuring up those memories kept me sane. But there was only one thing on my mind: when is this bloody war going to end? When are we going to get home? I knew I mustn't cave in, and should make the best of a bad thing, so I resolved to keep fit and exercise as much as possible, and also to try and keep myself clean, and not become totally lice-infested. My goal was to get home, no matter how long it took. My view was that having got away with my life when we crashed, why take a chance I'll die here?

After the Italians were taken out of the war, we were moved to Stalag IV-B in Germany, up in a place called Mühlberg, just east of the River Elbe. It was a bit grim, with an entrance like Auschwitz. It was an enormous camp, about twenty thousand people were there, although there was a typhus epidemic and thousands soon died. Every nationality in Europe seemed to be represented: French, Belgians, Serbs, Dutch, Italians, and about half of them were Russians. The Russians were treated worse than everyone else. I remember Russian prisoners of war coming into our Air Force compound – we Brits were kept in separate compounds for some reason – and going into the tip where the empty tins and all the other rubbish was dumped, and they put their hands in the tins and licked their fingers from sheer and utter deprivation and starvation.

There was horrible food at the Stalag, and little of it, because the Red Cross food parcels weren't coming through. We had a kind of ersatz coffee in the morning, boiled potatoes in their skins at lunch, and for dinner a soup which was essentially water, although occasionally it might have a bit of meat floating in it, or you might sometimes get a piece of cheese with caraway seeds.

We knew the Allies were getting nearer, because the Americans were bombing the railway line not far away. And then one morning we woke up and a brigade of Russians was outside; they were riding horses bareback, no saddles or reins. 'There's still fighting going on in the area,' they said, 'but you should go out and find your own food.' So we did go out and forage – the Nazi guards had either run away or been strung up by the Russians – and we caught a baby pig and butchered it, poor little thing, and several of us ate it.

American coaches came across the Elbe, and took us to Halle, in the suburbs of Berlin, where the American Air Force was stationed. We showered and were given clean clothes and then X-rayed. They then started to inspect everyone, one at a time: 'Right, *you're* clear.' '*You* can go home . . . ' I was not directed to go home. '*You've* got tuberculosis,' they said. So, here we go again . . . I was put in an RAF hospital and I convalesced there for over a year. People in those days were terrified of TB, and it was ages before even my parents came to see me.

For fifty years I never discussed any of this. I didn't want to bore anyone with it, and why would they be interested anyway? But when my grandson Richard was fourteen, he was given some project at school, and he said, 'Poppa, Poppa, what did you do in the war?' So I told him some of what I've told you, and he made quite a good story out of it. And then another grandchild asked me to tell her a story about the war, and now I've started writing down some of these tales. 'Poppa's Stories', I call them. Young people are very understanding. I often think it's easier to talk to your grandchildren than your own children, or even your wife sometimes.

I have a photographic memory, and even at ninety years old I can't delete some of the images, like the starving Russians, and poor old Graham, bobbing away in the sea. Fortunately, I very rarely dream about being a prisoner any more, just the odd nightmare: Oh God, I'm in a prisoner-of-war camp again, and it's not fair, it's not fair . . .

As far as my war effort, I was a dead loss; it must have cost thousands of pounds to train me as an RAF navigator, and they didn't get anything in return. I still feel a sense of guilt about that.

ART STACEY

Who's going to walk Sarah down the aisle . . . ?

I originally flew the Shackleton, which was a maritime patrol aircraft, four-engine, straight-wing. It was the last Second World War-type aircraft and always going wrong and leaking oil, with two engines on each wing, plus six contra-rotating propellers, which were very, very noisy. And, because of the endurance of the sorties, upwards of fourteen hours, when you lay in bed at night you could still hear the engines throbbing. I'm suffering now with high-term deafness and have to wear a hearing aid. Shack Ear, they call it.

So it was a quantum leap from the Shackleton to the Nimrod, an aircraft that was very advanced for its time. It was based on the Comet aircraft, which was the first jet passenger aircraft, when Britain still could build aircraft; it had a lovely, thin, tubular body, swept-back wings, which was novel for a civilian aircraft – such design qualities were usually the preserve of fighters and military aircraft – and long, very graceful undercarriage legs, which made the aircraft appear to be higher off the ground than it was.

I joined 51 Squadron in '91, and after four years I took over as pilot leader. 51 Squadron is a unique squadron in the RAF; it is a reconnaissance unit, tasked with gathering intelligence of various descriptions, but, primarily, the Nimrod was an ASW, an anti-submarine warfare aircraft, and our job was to detect, and, ultimately, in a war, destroy enemy submarines.

One day in May 1995 I looked at the programme for the following week and saw that I was scheduled to go to Kinloss to conduct an air test on one of our Nimrods.

The normal crew complement of a Nimrod is twenty-nine, which consists of two pilots, flight engineer, one navigator and twenty-five other guys of various trades and specialisations all jumbled up down the back – Russian speakers, Arabic speakers, you name it – but for the air test I took a minimum crew of seven.

We flew to Inverness in a civilian aircraft on the Monday.

Transport picked us up and drove us to the mess where we were given our rooms. I then unpacked, had a shower and rendezvoused at about six o'clock in the bar with the two other officers, had a pint before dinner, just a very quiet, relaxed evening, chatting away, and I stacked about 10.15 or so and went to bed.

Woke up the next morning, 16 May 1995, and it was a beautiful day, there wasn't a cloud in the sky, and just a gentle breeze, the gentlest of breezes.

We had a Met brief on what the weather was doing – there wasn't any. Although my plan was to land back at Kinloss, we chose Lossiemouth as our diversion airfield: when you fly, you always need to have an alternative landing point if anything were to happen to your landing point so you couldn't use it, like the weather clamps in and visibility deteriorates, or there are thunderstorms, or even a crash on the runway. Civilian pilots do that too.

I then briefed the crew, so they were all fully aware of what the mission was. We were taking off at 11 a.m. and planning to fly for four hours; the format of the sortie was that we would fly up to fifteen thousand feet, settle the aircraft down and then start the checks. At some stage we'd be climbing up to thirty-five thousand feet, where we'd be shutting engines down and relighting them, and working the flaps.

The co-pilot for the day was Flight Lieutenant Pat Hewitt, an ex-Rhodesian I'd known for years, and he was on the flight deck, switching on all the navigational aids, doing radio checks with the ground, preparing the cockpit, going through flaps with the engineer. Flight Sergeant David Rimmer, another good guy, was the flight engineer. The navigator was Flight Lieutenant Dick Chelu, lovely guy, one of life's characters.

I began doing external checks, looking round the aircraft, and after I signed the log to accept the aircraft from the ground engineers, I came forward and joined the co-pilot on the flight deck. I then went on the intercom: 'Crew, the captain is starting checks.' The three guys down the back as safety team were AEOp (Air Electronics Operator) Stu Clay, terrific guy, short and round as he is high, AEOp Andy Lawson, a big, tall fellow, with really stocky build, and the junior member of the crew was Sergeant Steve Hart. These guys had no active part in the air test; their job in the event of a problem, particularly under-floor problems like leaks or fumes, was to assist me in isolating, and, if necessary, fighting fire. More importantly, they were there to make the coffee, and keep it coming, because we were going to be pretty busy on the flight deck doing this air test.

The start-up was as per normal. I went through the starting cycle: started the engines in sequence, and then the engineer brought all the systems online and we began checking pressures and temperatures, and all the rest.

Eventually, we taxied out, got to the marshalling point and took off at two minutes to eleven. When we got airborne, it really was magnificent: you could see for a hundred miles in any direction. Kinloss, on the south coast of the Moray Firth, is a lovely part of the world, lots of wooded areas and mountains; you've got the Grampians to the south, and there was still a bit of snow on the peaks.

We climbed out and turned north up over the Moray Firth, and at fifteen thousand feet started checking bits and pieces as part of the air test. David Rimmer, the engineer, had the check-list on his lap, checking all four air-speed indicators were reading the same. The next thing Dave had to check was the engine anti-icing system. He started with number one engine, and watched the temperature rise, and switched it off. Same thing for number two, and number three. Number four was the one that caused us the problem.

Above number four engine was a collection of wires, and over the years, with the vibrations, the insulation that covers the wires had worn and, unbeknown to us, two wires were now touching: one of those wires went down to the engine anti-icing system, the other went down to the starter motor.

There was also another problem. An RAF ground engineer had been looking at the Rolls-Royce Spey engine that powered the Nimrods, and in particular a nut that held the turbine assembly within its titanium shroud, and this engineer was concerned about the strength of that nut; he reckoned if you put too much stress on it it would shatter, and if it did, the turbine assembly would be free to rotate itself off its mounting, and come into contact with the engine. And that could result in a catastrophic explosion.

In the flight safety world we talk about links in a chain that have to be formed before an accident happens, and with the touching wires, and the weakened nut, these were all forming . . .

When Dave Rimmer switched the power on to the fourth engine anti-icing system, the electrical current he sent down went to the starter motor with the weak nut. Down went that wiggly amp to tell the starter motor to start the engine. The air-starter valve on number four engine opened, and allowed air from an adjacent running engine on to the turbine assembly, and the turbine assembly inside was free to rotate as much as it liked, and so it went accelerating way up. The starter motor is designed to self-destruct at 107,000 revolutions per minute, which is a fair rate of acceleration, but it never got that far. All the pressure was exerted on that nut, and it shattered, and allowed the spinning turbine assembly to come out of its titanium shroud, and a four-inch piece of turbine blade went whistling, at supersonic speed, straight into the fuel tank alongside the number four engine, exploded inside and blew all the internal baffles that stop the fuel swishing out of the fuel tank, allowing the fuel to come pouring out on to the hot engine. When it hit the engine, an enormous explosion followed and the whole aircraft shuddered.

Fortunately, we hadn't yet used the fuel out of that tank: it's very hard to set fire to a liquid, it's only when it vaporises that you can ignite it ... two hours later, and that fuel tank would have been empty of fuel, and full of vapour, and any intrusion into a tank in that condition would have blown the wing off, and we would all have died, simple as that.

Meanwhile, Sergeant Steve Hart, one of the men in the safety team, was sent to look over the wing at number four engine: 'Grey smoke from the number four engine,' he said. But a few moments later, Steve came back with another report: 'Black smoke ...' Now, hold on, black smoke, that's fire ... Christ, this is a real emergency. I have to land.

I looked at the range on TACAN, a navigation system that tells you how far away you are from a beacon, and it was indicating we were forty-five miles from Kinloss, so flying time of about twelve to fifteen minutes. I started turning back towards Kinloss, where I intended to land.

But, suddenly, Steve reported flames coming from the number four engine. Unbeknown to us, the explosion also blew the engine covers from the underside of number four engine. So when we put the fire extinguishers into it, all they did was go straight overboard, which is why they didn't work. At the same time Dave Rimmer, the engineer, called out, 'Fire warning, zone two . . .' The fire had now spread down the engine to the rear half of the engine. Then Dave spoke again: 'Engine fire in number three,' so we shut that engine down as well, and, not to be outdone, Steve began reporting that flames were coming vertically out of the thrust reversers on the back of the engine, thousands of pounds of fuel were being driven out vertically at 350 miles an hour, and it was like a blowtorch. He was also reporting that panels were coming off the wing, just detaching themselves and disappearing off.

The co-pilot put his hand on the transmit switch and went, 'Mayday, Mayday, Mayday . . .' the international distress call, and informed Lossiemouth air traffic of our problem: 'We've got double engine fire on numbers three and four, and we're returning to Kinloss for an emergency landing . . .'

What we had to do now was dump fuel, because we'd taken off with enough fuel for four hours, about twenty-five tons, and I would have to dump about half that to get down to any form of landing weight, otherwise that would put too much stress on the undercarriage.

We needed to get down as soon as possible. Time was of the essence.

I was descending at 300 knots, or 350 miles an hour. At this stage, I could see Kinloss, but in my path was Lossiemouth, my alternative destination, and ten miles closer than Kinloss, plus Kinloss runway is east-west and Lossiemouth is north-south: I was coming in from a northerly direction, so Lossiemouth was perfectly lined up for that runway, and could save me two or three minutes. I told air traffic that my intention was now to divert to Lossiemouth for an emergency landing.

There wasn't one split second where I suddenly thought, We've got to ditch. It was a gradual process of thinking, how much longer have I got to stay airborne? How long do I need to reach the runway at Lossiemouth? And how long are my wings going to last? Because I thought it was not going to be too long before the flames were going to reach the fuel tank, and blow our wings off; maybe minutes, maybe seconds.

It was at that stage I started to favour the ditching option.

The ditching option is not a great one; but if you've got no other option you have to do it. Old [Chesley] Sullenberger did a wonderful job when he ditched in the Hudson; I've got every admiration for that guy. I would not like to have attempted what he did with an aircraft with underslung engines, but he touched both engines at exactly the same time, so they acted as skids. Had he touched one lower than the other, the aircraft would have gone over and over, and they would all have died. I didn't have that particular problem, because the Nimrod engines are built into the wing, so it was almost like a boat underneath. All I had to do was keep the wings level. Also, trying to ditch when you've got swell is suicidal, your chances of survival are remote, but on this particular day the weather was still perfect, and the sea was like a millpond. So everything was in my favour. I said to the crew, 'Crew, we are ditching the aircraft, prepare the aircraft for ditching.'

The correct procedure for ditching a Nimrod is to land at VaT, velocity at threshold, which is a function of the aircraft weight, minus ten knots, which is the speed that prevents you stalling. I levelled the aircraft at a thousand feet, and throttled back to let the speed wash off. We got to about 220 knots, and I said, 'Right, Pat, give me twenty flap.' But the flap didn't move: the hydraulic system that controls the flaps had been fed into the fire. 'OK,' I said, 'we will ditch flapless,' which really was rash; no one had ever contemplated ditching a Nimrod flapless. I then declared we would ditch at 125 knots, which was an arbitrary figure but just seemed a suitable speed for the circumstances.

We continued down.

At seven hundred feet I ordered all the crew to take up ditching positions, and, because I couldn't see down the back, I asked Steve Hart for a final report on the wing.

'Skipper, the wing is melting.'

I finally brought the airbrakes in with the last of the residual pressure and prepared for the ditching, getting the speed right and concentrating on keeping my wings level with the horizon. It became very hard in the latter stages to judge height, because the sea was so calm; there were no wavelets to give any idea of height.

Finally I was level with the lighthouse at Lossiemouth. The sun was shining on it, and it was painted white, like a wedding cake. As it happens, my eldest daughter, Sarah, was due to get married in a few months and you can imagine in our house there was all the preparation for the wedding – flowers, wedding dresses and so on. Suddenly, the thought went through my mind, Who's going to walk Sarah down the aisle if I don't make it? And it came to me, Ray – my brother-in-law – he'll do it. Problem solved.

Now concentrate on the ditching, Art.

We came down and down, and then we hit. Because I was flapless, it was quite a high-nose attitude, so I hit the water hard. The noise of the aircraft hitting the sea at 140 to 150 miles per hour is indescribable, you've never heard anything louder or more terrifying: the sound of the actual impact is explosive, then you've got things detaching themselves, plus the noise of the sea hammering on the front of the aircraft . . .

The deceleration started as soon as we touched the water. We had inertia reels, but Pat, with a thousand and one things to do, had forgotten to check that my seat was in the locked position, and the shoulder harnesses had been locked. So, as the aircraft started decelerating, I began pivoting forward, and the instrument panel came up fast, and I thought, my face and head are going to smash into it. And as I turned my head away, I reckoned, This is it, this is how you'll go . . . I got to about nine inches away when the inertia reels of my harness clicked in and pulled me back – and I then hit the seat full blast. My head went back so fast, and with such force, that had the headrest not been there my neck would have snapped. Fortunately, about two years before, they'd fitted headrests on the seats. I started going forward once more. Not again, I thought. But this time I only went forward about three or four inches, then stopped.

The aircraft bounced twice, and then slewed through eighty degrees until it eventually stopped. And it was silent then, really silent, after all the noise. And then there was the realisation . . . Christ, you're still alive. I looked across at the co-pilot, and Pat was moving, he was starting to unstrap, so I thought, Well, that's two of us. I then looked behind me, and the engineer was getting out of his seat. That's three of us who have made it.

Andy Lawson, the big fellow, had been down the back. The seats are on tracks, and during the ditching these tracks had distorted and allowed his seat to come out, with the result that when we decelerated he was propelled down the aircraft, together with his seat still attached to his backside, and ended up with his head and shoulders wedged in one of the panels that had come loose in the aircraft floor, a panel now full of fuel and seawater. Stu Clay, the littlest person on board, saw what had happened and as soon as we came to a halt he rushed forward to where Andy Lawson was like a cork in the top of a bottle, and literally picked him up righted him, and helped him to get out of the seat. That's adrenaline for you: the amount of adrenaline that was pumping round enabled him to lift a fifteen-stone man, wringing wet, plus his seat.

My headset had gone, so I could no longer speak to the crew, so at the top of my voice I shouted, 'Everybody out!' although I don't think they needed any bidding. By this time, there was about a foot of water in the cockpit, and the smell of fuel was getting strong, and the aircraft was groaning and creaking. All I could think was that we must get away from this aircraft as quickly as possible, because there's hot metal all around, and any minute we could have an explosion. I started wading through the water, got about two or three paces and became aware that I'd injured my back.

There was a large dinghy in each wing root, which is where the wing joins the fuselage, but unfortunately the starboard one had been burnt away by the fire, and the port one, for some unknown reason, had inflated itself during the ditching and been ripped away from its mountings and was floating upside down about a quarter of a mile away. Fortunately, we'd got an extra dinghy internally stowed, so the boys put that out on to the wing, and when they pulled the lanyard it unravelled like a snake. So we piled into the dinghy, and I did a quick head count ... seven. We'd all survived. Andy Lawson was bleeding and the engineer had gashed his hand in the ditching, so there was blood all over the place, but everyone else seemed to be OK.

The next thing we heard was a helicopter arriving; it was there within minutes. Actually, it turns out that the helicopter, a Sea King, was already airborne when we ditched, because it was doing a practice run with someone who was filming on RAF rescue techniques. Down came the winchman on the end of the wire, and landed right on our dinghy. 'Good morning gentlemen,' he

said. 'Like a lift anywhere?' Yeah, did we ever! Someone said, 'The skipper's hurt his back.' 'Right, back injury? I'll take the skipper up first.' So the old idea of the captain being the last one to leave the ship went by the board, and he took me up first into the helicopter, and brought the others up two by two, and within ten minutes we were all onboard.

We were taken to Lossiemouth. A doctor met the helicopter, did the initial assessment, and said, 'Right, these three for hospital,' meaning Andy Lawson, Dave Rimmer and me. The helicopter then got airborne to Dr Gray's Hospital in Elgin, the nearest town. We landed in the grounds there, and I was given a neck brace, put in a wheelchair and was taken off to A&E, and within minutes lots of people were around me cutting off my flying suit, needles were stuck in arms to check blood pressures, and all that sort of rubbish.

I was not impressed with Dr Gray's. Someone took an X-ray of my back and had a quick look. 'Can't see any injuries,' he said. Well, how come I've got this pain in my lower back? Fortunately, within two hours, a specialist orthopaedic man came and looked at the X-ray and said, 'Your back's broken.'

Andy had sustained quite a lot of injuries: broken ribs, a broken ankle, both ears perforated and a back injury like myself, which they failed to diagnose. In that first critical twenty-four hours, he should have been carefully monitored, but he was allowed to walk around with a broken back, with the result that his injuries were long-term, and he never did return to flying. He was medically discharged from the Air Force and now walks with a stick.

They operated on David Rimmer's broken finger three times

in twenty-four hours because they couldn't get it right. He was finally discharged and went home.

So that left just Andy and me. I rang up the squadron and said, 'Get us out of here.' And that day an RAF helicopter took us down to a military hospital in Holton, and the next night we were under RAF doctors, and a wonderful orthopaedic surgeon.

I was released the following week and ambulanced home. The neighbours had put bunting all over the house, and Val, my wonderful wife, was waiting for me. I was home. I was on sick leave for about three months, and then eventually they said, 'How do you feel about returning to flying?' And I said 'Why not?' And I went back flying.

Touch wood, I've never had a flashback about the ditching, I've never had a nightmare about it, maybe because I didn't see the fire. At least one of the crew received counselling for years and years after the event.

I can't say I've changed because of what happened. But I do appreciate things a lot more now, and I've always considered the years since 16 May 1995 to have been a bonus. I suppose it could have been my day of death.

Sarah's wedding was wonderful, and very emotional. She had asked me to wear uniform, so I wore my number ones, and they played Elgar's 'Nimrod' as she and I walked down the aisle, and that's a beautiful bit of music which I must admit always brings tears to my eyes.

Normally the bride's father does his speech, then the groom and then the best man. I made my speech, and all I did extra was to say how delighted and grateful I was to be there. But then suddenly Sarah stood up, which was completely unexpected, because she's actually quite shy. Even Val didn't know this was going to happen, and I don't think her husband-to-be knew. 'I want to say a few words about my dad,' she said, and she went on about how grateful she was that her father was there to give her away. Oh, it was very moving, I must admit.

One more thing. All the lads from the plane were there too: they bought a set of tumblers as a present, and on each of the glasses they'd had engraved 'To Sarah: From Art's Crash Test Dummies'.

In November of that year I was called into the squadron boss's office, and he said, 'Congratulations, Art, I'm to advise you that you've been awarded an Air Force Cross . . .' which is one of the highest awards you can receive in peacetime.

That was organised for February '96, and I went to Buckingham Palace with Val and the two girls. It varies who hands out the medals, but it was the Queen on that particular day, which was wonderful.

There's a man in full Household uniform with a tray of medals and awards standing next to the Queen; your name is called – I think the exact words were, 'Flight Lieutenant Stacey, to be awarded the Air Force Cross.' I've actually got a video somewhere, which I bought at a vast price. The ADC then whispers to the Queen something like, 'This is the Nimrod pilot,' just as a refresher, although I'm sure she will have read the brief. She's like that.

And suddenly there's the Queen on a platform in front of you, and she's looking at you. You bow your head, march forward about three or four paces, you stop, and then she pins on the medal; well, it's Velcro, in fact.

And then she said something like, 'Congratulations on the

award we followed your exploits with interest,' although to be honest I can't remember the exact words, I was so ruddy nervous. She asked how I was, and I said I was back flying now. 'What about the rest of the crew?' and I said, 'All but one, we've all returned to flying.' 'That's wonderful news,' she said. And then she said: 'It was a wonderful thing you did.'

And at that stage she's got the mental clock going; she knows we've had twelve seconds, or whatever, and she holds out her hand, you very gently take it, shake it, and then you step back about three paces, bow your head, turn around and march off. The medal is immediately taken from you, it's boxed, and then given back to you later.

To be honest, it was such an overwhelming affair, plus there was added hoopla because it was the same day that Elton John got his knighthood. All in all, I found it far more nerve-racking than the ditching. At least with the ditching I was in control; at the awards ceremony I wasn't. But it was a wonderful day, and all three girls, Val, Sarah and Nicky, were in tears.

FRED HART

'You little devil, Fred . . . '

In 1947 I was a ground engineer in the RAF. I had been in Palestine for eighteen months with the Airborne Support Squadron. Palestine was a beautiful land; most of it was covered in orange groves, and they used to grow everything you could think of: grapes, grapefruit and massive watermelons. In fact, it would have been a perfect posting if there hadn't been the problems with the Stern Gang, so you couldn't go anywhere without having a gun with a bullet up the spout, all waiting and ready, and you had to sleep with your gun beside the bed.

My squadron was disbanded, and because I was a regular, not a national serviceman, I had to stay in the Middle East to finish my tour. I was posted down to Egypt, and joined 216 Squadron at Kibrit in the Canal Zone, which was a cushy billet compared to Palestine. Kibrit was at the eastern end of the Great Bitter Lake, and we had a private beach within the bounds of the camp; we used to work early mornings until early afternoon, and then we had the rest of the afternoon off, so after lunch you could just take your towel and swimsuit down to the beach.

Dakotas made up the main part of the transport squadrons of the Middle East. They didn't regularly have flight engineers on the Dakotas, but when they had to fly to airfields where there were no service facilities then they took one of us with them as part of the crew. Well, the squadron was flying all over the Middle East at that time, and we were always keen to fly with them because it was exciting to get away from camp. They used to do a weekly run from Egypt down to Nairobi, and they operated a slip crew then: you'd fly down there and the crew that was already there would bring that aircraft back, and it would be another week until the next aircraft arrived, so you had a week's holiday. That was the one trip everyone wanted to do. Eventually, the opportunity came up to go on one of those flights, and they asked if I would like to go with it. To which I replied, I most certainly would.

We had ten passengers on the flight, a mixture of Army and RAF, plus one civilian lady, who was a representative of something called the Malcolm Club, which was a club for wounded airmen, started by Lady Malcolm, who had lost all her sons in the war.

We took off on 27 June 1947. We landed first at Wadi Halfa, on the River Nile, to refuel. Then on to Khartoum to refuel again, and we stayed the night there because it was late afternoon by then and we couldn't fly at night, which was just safety regulations, as we were carrying passengers who weren't carrying parachutes, and, if anything went wrong, we couldn't very well jump out and leave them aboard.

We took off from Khartoum quite early in the morning, heading for Juba in southern Sudan, which was the last refuelling stop before Nairobi. About an hour or so into the flight, we had to go slightly off course and climb to twelve thousand feet to get away from some cumulonimbus, when there was a knock on the flight compartment door. The navigator opened the door, and one of the passengers, an RAF sergeant, said, 'Excuse me, no panic, but I think the starboard wing is on fire.'

Because of the shape of the wings, we couldn't actually see it from the cockpit – you could only see it through the windows of the fuselage – so I went back with the navigator to have a look. And, sure enough, you could see flames coming over the leading edge of the wing just on the outboard side of the starboard engine. The pilot then came back to have a look, 'Right,' he said, 'I'll switch off the engine and set off the fire extinguishers', which he did. But that didn't put the fire out. Then he said, 'I'll put the aircraft into a dive, to see if I can blow it out,' which didn't work either. And after that he decided he would have to terminate the flight, and the wireless op began to send out Maydays.

We told the passengers what was happening, and, if anyone was worried, they didn't show it: there was no noise, nobody was screaming, like you see on television dramas.

When we broke below the cloud, we were on the edge of Lake Kielger in the northern part of Uganda, and there were swamps everywhere; in that part of the world there are swamps that go on for hundreds of miles.

The seating arrangement in the Dakota at that time was long

canvas benches down each side of the fuselage, because it was all set up for parachute jumping. The passengers were sitting five a side, and we told them to link arms with each other, the idea being they'd be better able to absorb any bumps when we landed.

I sat down behind the pilot, but I didn't have any straps so I just had to hope for the best, put my faith in the pilot bringing the aircraft in smoothly, although when you're about to ditch you can't help but wonder if you're going to come out of it.

But he actually did a lovely landing; when he was just about to land, he switched off the other engine and feathered the props. The aircraft went into the water, but because a Dakota is nice and clean underneath the main planes, there's no obstructions, and it was just like a glider going in. Then the water itself stopped us, and we tipped up a bit on the nose.

Well, as soon as it stopped, I grabbed the fire extinguisher and began climbing up to go out of the hatch, but the pilot turned to me and said, 'Where on earth do you think you're going with that?'

'I'm going to put the fire out.'

'Don't be daft,' he said, 'the water's already done that.' So I came back in and put the fire extinguisher away.

By that time, the navigator had thrown away the emergency door and started throwing out the dinghies. The first one he threw out collapsed; it was a dud. But as luck would have it, there were still three five-man dinghies, enough to cater for all of us, with ten passengers and five crew. We got the passengers into the dinghies, and I was the last one out of the aircraft, and I grabbed the fire axe, which I thought might be useful. By rights, I shouldn't have taken it into the dinghies, because there was a possibility it could damage them, but it was a good job I did because all the dinghies were tied to the aircraft, and I had to chop the cords, otherwise we would have gone down with the plane.

It took about four minutes for the aircraft to disappear. We just sat there, and watched our plane gradually filling with water, getting heavier and heavier, and finally sinking. The last bit to go down was the tail, the fin and the rudder. We all felt a bit sad to see the old plane go.

We tried to paddle our dinghies, but we couldn't make much headway across a thick expanse of lily pads, and, besides, we didn't know which direction to go. After maybe an hour or so, we suddenly saw some natives coming towards us in dugout canoes; they must have seen us or heard us come down. They were all standing up and paddling like hell, and they were pretty much naked, although most of them had a cloth over their shoulders.

The passengers went into the dugout canoes, and the natives took the rest of us in tow, until we got to their village, which was quite far away. There was a little pathway through the jungle to the lake, and women were carrying water containers on their heads as they went to the lake to get water, and they just had loincloths, with nothing on the top, which distracted my attention, because there were some very beautiful-looking women there, with lovely figures, and, well, I was only a lad of nineteen.

We spread out everything we had in yellow, which is a very conspicuous colour, including our Mae Wests, in a patch of clearing, to try to make us obvious from the air. We had a portable wind-up radio that could send out messages. You had to do this at ten minutes to the hour, and ten minutes after the hour, which is the emergency time for everyone in the world, and every aircraft flying was supposed to listen in at those times, although I don't think anybody ever did.

The natives were standing around, watching us, interested in everything we were doing, but couldn't really do anything now to help, but fortunately one young native turned up who could speak a bit of English, because he'd been to a mission school, and he said there was a government agricultural experimental station a few miles away. He had a bicycle with no tyres or seat, although I remember it had a little enamel badge on the handlebars which said *Made in Birmingham*, and our pilot gave him a message to take to the station, while we carried on sending out the messages.

It must have been about four o'clock when a truck appeared from the experimental station, and we all got in the truck and left everything for the natives to do what they wanted with them, although I wished afterwards I had kept my Mae West, as it would have been a nice memento.

Anyway, they took us to Serolti, which was the nearest habitable town, if you could call it a town. All the locals and the white people had heard about us, and were gathered in the clubhouse, and everybody had drinks there. And then all the crew went to a government resthouse and native staff looked after us. They cooked a lovely dinner for us that night, Lancashire Hotpot. I don't know what kind of meat they added to it, but we found out afterwards that the swamp we landed in was infested with crocodiles, so I am hoping it wasn't crocodile.

When Nairobi heard we were safe, they sent a Dakota to pick us up the following day. We all piled into the plane, but, with it being such a small airstrip, everyone had to go up to the nose and crush into the pilot's compartment to get the weight forward, then we had to belt the engines like hell and just hope we could take off at the end of this short airstrip before we hit the trees, which we did, and we all sat down after that with a big sigh of relief.

When we got to Nairobi, the passengers all dispersed to do what they had to do, but we crew were there for a week, and we went nearly every night into Nairobi and had a rip-roaring time, all boys together, and we'd have a good drink and a singsong.

They had a Board of Inquiry to satisfy the authorities what had happened to our plane, but they didn't find out what had caused it and the aircraft is at the bottom of the swamp, so probably no one will ever know. My opinion is that one of the fuel lines going into the engine itself may have come undone, or broken, and caught fire from the engine, so setting off the fire extinguishers wouldn't have put it out. Actually, the fire was burning very close to the fuel tanks, and if it had got any closer, well, we'd have all gone, and I wouldn't be here today.

I didn't tell the family for such a long time about my ditching; well, we'd got children, and life was full of so many other things. I told my wife in about 1987, and my sister in Gosport, who's ninety-three now, I told her only a few years ago, and she turned to me and said, 'You little devil, Fred.'

I don't know what's happened since to the chaps I flew with on that flight. I checked the records with the Goldfish Club in case any of them had joined, but they haven't. People die off, of course, although I'm eighty-four at the moment, and still going strong, apart from getting to the point where I can't walk very far without falling over, and I had a bad fall about two weeks ago. But I feel lucky to be here, and I try to live a normal life, although my wife died about three years ago and I miss her every day.

My wife would never go to any of my service reunions. She used to say, 'Well, that's your thing, Fred, you go and enjoy yourself.' I always wished she would come, because she'd have met a lot of people, and especially with the Goldfish Club, they're such lovely people. In a way I'm glad I ditched because it gave me the opportunity to be a member of a unique association. The Goldfish Club is such a marvellous thing. I missed our reunion this year, because it had to be cancelled as they didn't get a good response from the members; well, there's not many of us left, you see. I'd hate to think it's going to collapse.

I think about my ditching quite a lot, particularly when I'm in bed and trying to get off to sleep, it all goes through my mind. But it doesn't upset me. I think it calms my nerves.

GORDON CHAMBERS

'I come from working-class people . . .'

After the war almost every teenager joined a cadet force of some sort. I went in the Air Cadets at about fifteen, because my brother Keith, who was two years older, had been in before me. And then as soon as your eighteenth birthday was passed anybody who had two legs was conscripted.

I became an air mechanic, or FME, Flight Mechanic Engines, and was posted to Topcliffe in Yorkshire to service aircraft that were being used in the Berlin Airlift of June 1948 to May 1949. They were big four-engine aircraft, Avro Yorks and Hastings; some of the Yorks were flying in bags of coal, and after servicing one of those you came out as black as your hat. We were there two or three months until the airlift finished, and then I got this overseas posting to Gibraltar, which was wonderful, as I'd never been out of the country before.

We formed up into proper marching units on Liverpool Docks, and as we marched along the jetty we came up to this boat in front of us, a beautiful black and white Cunard ship called the *Georgic*, and we all thought: This is our boat, blooming marvellous. But they marched us straight past it, and there was this grey tub – everything was painted grey except for the name, *Empress of Britain*, which was painted black. It was a captured German supply ship, an absolute wreck of a thing. It took about four days to get to Gibraltar through the Bay of Biscay, and it was rough going, to say the least.

In Gibraltar we had to service four old Halifax Mk6 bombers which had been converted for air-sea rescue, and a couple of single-engine planes that were used for target-towing for the fleet to shoot at, and an Anson C19, which was the Air Officer Commander's personal plane. When there was a big parade to celebrate, he would use it to come and take the salute, and it had also been converted for air-sea rescue service, but it mostly just stood there and didn't get used much; it always had its engine covers on.

There is only one runway at Gib, which was built across a

road, and they would close the road when the planes came in. It's quite an iffy place to get in and out of, especially when there's crosswinds. The runway wasn't really long enough: if you ran out of runway east to west, you went into the Bay of Algeciras, and if you ran over flying west to east, you would come down in the Med. Sometimes the weather got so foul you would just have to close down, and then people would fly on to an American naval airbase in Morocco, which was just a short hop.

On Friday morning, 9 March, we were going to Lisbon to service a Halifax that was stuck there. We took off, and flew straight into what we would now call a bird strike. I learned afterwards that the Spanish had recently opened a sardine factory, and there were huge flocks of seagulls everywhere, and some had gone into our carburettor intakes. When we came down, I reported to the flight sergeant that I was available for work, and he said, 'Don't unpack your bag, come down at half-past seven tomorrow.'

So I went down with my bag in the morning, and there was the Commander's Anson, with my mate Benson setting it all up. It was his pride and joy actually.

The pilot was Flying Officer Wilson, a navigator, Flying Officer Ferguson, who was also the second pilot, and a radio operator, a French Canadian called Flight Lieutenant La Belle, a long-service man who had been in the Royal Canadian Air Force for the whole of the war and then taken commission into the RAF. Sergeant Dobbs was there to do the engines, and Flying Officer Miller, who I had never seen before, was the ground engineer.

The sun was shining and the weather was clear when we took off for the second time to service the Halifax in Lisbon.

Because of the political differences between England and Spain over who owned Gibraltar, we weren't allowed to overfly Spanish territory, so we had to fly outside the twelve-mile limit along the coast of Spain. We had been out an hour and a half, and were heading north up the coast, when we encountered this storm, a huge wall of dark, mucky-looking clouds. I had never seen weather conditions like it, and I remember Sergeant Dobbs saying, 'Now, *that's* what you call a storm front . . .'

We weren't flying very high, maybe three thousand feet, and I said to Dobbsy, 'I hope we are going to fly over it, because we won't be able to fly under it', because it went right down to the sea. But suddenly we were in it, and it was a violent storm, and threw us about all over the place, and I got really badly airsick, God, it knocked me out. There was a kind of stowage area at the rear of the aircraft, where I saw the engine covers, which were quite clean and nicely folded up, so I had a lie-down on them. I don't know how long I was there, I must have dozed off – it was quite exhausting being that sick – until Sergeant Dobbs tapped me on my shoulder, and said, 'Can you get back to your seat? We are going in.' Those were his exact words. I thought, Oh good, we are at Lisbon, but I looked out of the window and the plane was in a steep banking turn, and all I could see was the sea. La Belle said to me and Dobbs, 'Sit with your back against the bulkhead partition.' And just as well he did, because one second later the plane turned round and hit the sea.

If you go into an orderly room on almost any Air Force base you will see diagrams of ditching procedure, but you can't practise ditching really, can you? You just have to do it. The technique is to turn the plane into the wind, so you have got maximum air speed, and as you fly over water you get almost within touching distance, and then the pilot pulls the nose up sharp, so the back half of the aeroplane hits the sea at an angle and takes off all your forward speed, and then finally he just drops the nose and you are floating.

Wilson did a good job of landing, but, because of the waves and the wind and driving rain, the pilot and the navigator took a fair old jolt, and Miller fell forward out of his seat and sprawled on the floor, but he wasn't hurt and got back in his seat. With my back against the bulwark, as La Belle had suggested, I didn't feel the impact.

Theoretically, the captain of the aircraft should have been in charge of procedure now. La Belle knew what he was doing, and he organised everything. There was water coming into the front of the plane, you could see it running along the floor, and Mr La Belle marshalled the pilot and the navigator out through the escape hatch, and out on to the wing, then he motioned to Dobbsy and me, and he passed us the valise the main dinghy was in, which was a big canvas bag with two handles on it, and laced up with a toggle. 'Keep your hand on this toggle,' he said, 'but don't pull it until I tell you.'

Now this is a bit distressing. Flying Officer Miller wouldn't get out of his seat. He had lost his bottle, and was screaming at the top of his voice: 'Somebody help me.' It was constant: 'Help me, help me, help me . . . ' I had never seen anybody lose it like that. But by now the plane had filled up with water, and there was nothing La Belle could do. Finally, La Belle came out. He had been sending Mayday signals, and didn't leave his position until the water was too high for him to stay.

So now there were five of us in the water, holding this dinghy, which was only partially inflated. The dinghy had ropes to hang on to inside and out, and La Belle went swimming round to all of us, positioning people so we were evenly spaced around the dinghy. Flying Officer Wilson got his foot caught through one of the guy ropes, and turned upside down in the water, but La Belle sorted him out.

Then La Belle came back to me and said, 'Reach down and take your shoes off, because you can't climb into a dinghy in shoes.' I mean, it would have been a disaster if somebody had gone through the canvas, wouldn't it?

Eventually he said, 'Pull the toggle.' So I pulled the toggle, but within a few seconds the plane's tail came up while we were standing on the wing and threw the five of us into the water, which was bloody cold, I can tell you, although fortunately we were in life jackets, because you wore those all the time you were flying. And then, as the tail of the plane went down, it just touched the dinghy – if it had been fully inflated I think it would have taken it down.

It was a bit difficult to get into the dinghy, because there was still quite a swell on, but La Belle organised that too: he said he would push me upwards when I heaved the top of my body on to the side of the dinghy, which he did. Then, when I was in, he said, 'Now lie down in the dinghy for a minute', and he went round and got all the people in the dinghy to pull up the people who weren't in.

Everyone looked OK, except Ferguson, who had a bit of Perspex stuck in his thigh and was looking as white as a sheet. I was wondering, Why doesn't that bleed? But eventually I realised it didn't bleed because the water was so damn cold.

We all thought that Miller had gone down with the plane, as he was in his seat at the very last minute, but suddenly he appeared. He was not more than ten yards away from us in the water, still in his seat, which had been torn away from the plane. I can still see his expression: it was wild, with his face all red and his mouth wide open, and his eyes staring, shouting constantly, 'Somebody help me, somebody help me, somebody help me . . .'

Mr La Belle tried to throw a rope to Miller, but it wouldn't reach, and he actually got back in the water and tried to swim to him, but it was impossible, the waves were so high, and, with the force of the wind as well, within a minute or two the sea just took Mr Miller out and we lost sight of him completely.

We pulled La Belle back in and he organised us again, and moved people around. He put this Walter set between my legs, and said, 'Hold on to this, and crank it.' This was an orange plastic emergency radio that was part of the survival equipment – why it was called Walter, I don't know. It had two terminals on the top, and when you hand-cranked it you were turning the dynamo, which would automatically send a locating signal.

Anyway, La Belle made me turn this bloody thing for half an hour with one arm, and then half an hour with the other. I was actually falling asleep occasionally, because I was exhausted physically, but La Belle would just wake me up and make me wind it again. I learned afterwards that there was another bag that went with it which carried the aerial. In fact, without the aerial, there was no way there was going to be a signal coming out of that thing, and I now realise he was making me do it to keep me warm, because I was soaking wet and very, very cold – four hours in the Atlantic in March ain't fun.

We were sitting in what was a huge dirty green saucer and we were blowing about all over the place. We had left the distress flares and paddles on the plane; there hadn't been time to get them. One moment you couldn't see out when you were in the trough of the waves, and then the lip of a wave would turn over, and, as it came under you, *whoosh*, suddenly you were thirty feet up in the air, and you could see for miles, even though it was murky. At times we could see ships on the horizon, and it isn't an exaggeration to say we were almost run down by a fishing vessel that was heading for port. We could even see the captain with his nose up against his windscreen. We were all shouting at him, but there was no way he could have heard us, it was very noisy – gale force winds, you see.

At about four o'clock we were found by a French destroyer called the *Marceau*. They turned around to shelter us, but the rise and fall of the water meant that getting off the dinghy on to the ship was quite a hairy operation. But La Belle organised that too, because he could talk to them in French.

They sent down two rope ladders as far down as they could go, which wasn't all that far, with a sailor on each. I was balancing on the side of the dinghy, with La Belle supporting me, and he said, 'Now, jump when I tell you . . .' and I jumped when we bobbed up towards the ladder, and these two matelots grabbed me and pulled me up. I was then simply picked up by this one great big sailor, absolutely huge bloke he was, carried away and stripped, rubbed down with towels, put in a bunk and covered with blankets. And a little while afterwards, this bloke came back and spooned hot soup into me.

They had this emergency clothing they gave us, so when I

came off the *Marceau* in Gibraltar I was in a matelot's gear. I had their sailors' trousers, which were not so bell-bottomed as ours, a big blue sweater and espadrilles, and underwear that was incredibly itchy.

About an hour or two after we were on board, a French officer came round and said they had found Miller's body, and that he was dead.

That whole situation with Miller affected me quite a lot. You see, I come from working-class people, and until then I thought all officers were marvellous, officers and gentlemen, and all of that, and when I realised they could have feet of clay, it shook my confidence a bit.

Because of the loss of the aeroplane, and the loss of life, there was a Board of Inquiry that we had to attend. The accident was blamed on pilot error, because Flying Officer Wilson didn't divert when he should have done. In bad weather we should have diverted to Cadiz, but Flying Officer Wilson tried to go across the strait to Tangier, and there wasn't enough fuel. Wilson had a loss of seniority, and was reprimanded, which is no more than a slap on the wrist. I was told that I was not to speak about Flying Officer Miller, because it would upset his family. They also said they would be recommending Flight Lieutenant La Belle for an award; well, it was quite obvious we would not have survived if it had not been for him.

Well, my ditching story is not an achievement, is it? Quite the opposite, in fact. On that afternoon I was just frozen with fear, and I am conscious of the fact that I survived, but contributed nothing to the fact that I survived both in the plane or in the sea. La Belle did it all. We would not have survived but for him, there's no doubt about that.

I had signed up for five years in the RAF altogether, but after that I wanted to finish my time and get out. I worked for an engineering company in the town when I came out, and then I did teacher training and taught engineering at a local college, until I retired when I was seventy-five. I'm now eighty-one.

SIR RICHARD BRANSON

'Richard, where are you? . . . '

I've crash landed in the desert, and a number of times in various other places – over ten times in all – and I've ditched into the sea twice: once when we attempted to cross the Atlantic in a hot-air balloon, and on to an icy lake the other time. The lake was in the Arctic, when we were doing the Trans-Pacific crossing, and that was certainly the most drawn-out episode of them all, and the most terrifying.

The Trans-Pacific came after the Trans-Atlantic ditching. My friend Per Lindstrand and I thought we could learn from all the mistakes and go on to the next big challenge, and, obviously, the next big challenge was the Pacific. We should have learned our lessons from the Atlantic and called it a day but, boys being boys, we didn't.

We built this gigantic balloon: you could stack ten 747s on top of each other inside it, it was awesomely big. We went to a place called Miyakonojo, right at the very southern tip of Japan, chosen because the jet stream travels over it extremely quickly. Actually, that's where they set off thousands of little balloons with incendiary devices during the Second World War, to try to set fire to American forests and cities, so at least we knew that some balloons had managed to cross the Pacific before.

Finally, on one very chilly morning in November 1989, we were ready to leave. About thirty thousand Japanese children and their parents were all huddled together, waving little Japanese flags and waiting to watch the balloon take off. But, just moments before we boarded, the whole outer casing of the balloon collapsed on top of the burners because frost had got into the balloon. We were fortunate still to be on the ground when it happened, because we would have been in really serious trouble if we'd been in the air. So we had to apologise to the crowd and tell them we were obviously not going to be able to take off that day, and that we'd be back again the following year.

We came out again in January 1991, again on a freezing cold

morning, and this time something like a hundred thousand people turned up. The departure date had been delayed, and during that time I took my family away to a little island off Japan. There was a Japanese balloonist who had attempted to beat us to it, and as we were coming through the airport television screens were showing news pictures of his body being pulled out of the sea by a helicopter, so having been euphoric about the trip, that cast a sombre cloud over it. But we decided to continue, so we said our good-byes, climbed into the balloon and took off.

The first thousand miles went really well. Getting into the jet stream is always exciting because you're flying in winds that are a hundred miles an hour after you've been going maybe ten miles an hour, and it's like being dragged along by ten thousand horses. A Force 8 gale was blowing across the Pacific – really strong winds – and even though we were flying at thirty-five thousand feet we could see the waves churning below us, and under no circumstances would we have wanted to ditch in that.

About twelve hundred miles into the trip we strapped ourselves in to release the first empty fuel tank, but as we jettisoned it something went horribly wrong. We couldn't work out exactly what had happened, but the whole capsule lurched to one side: Per disappeared about six feet below me, and I shot up six feet above where we had been. I looked at the stream that was following the empty capsule going towards the sea and three other capsules – about 60 per cent of our fuel – were going with it, with the remainder of our fuel dangling precariously from one side of the capsule.

We immediately grasped the implications of this: we had insufficient fuel to complete the journey, or to turn back, and therefore we had to assume we would be forced to ditch into the sea at some stage in the next twenty-four to thirty hours, and that the chances of us surviving were almost non-existent. It was among the most uncomfortable few moments of my life.

Furthermore, we had a conversation with our base in Los Angeles, and they started talking to ships, but all the ships they spoke with said the weather was so bad there was no way they could pick anyone up to make a rescue. Also, about a day into the trip, we'd got a message that the Gulf War had broken out. Bombing had started, so we knew there would be very little help if we ended up in the sea as everyone would be preoccupied with that, so things were pretty bleak.

However, after we got over the initial shock we did some calculations and worked out that if we were to cross the Pacific with the remaining fuel we would have to average about 180 miles an hour. The fastest a balloon had ever gone was 110 mph, so our only chance was to fly the balloon right into the core of the jet stream and see if we could find winds that would give us the kind of speed we needed. And remarkably, watching the speedometer, I saw we were going 110 mph, 120, 130, 150, 160, 170 mph, and then I saw it hitting 200 mph. We managed to find a stream that actually took us up to 220 at some stages, and once we even hit 245 mph. I'm not a religious person, but I could have become one on that trip.

The absolute key was for Per and I to stay awake for the next two or three days, and 100 per cent concentrating. We had to make sure that we always watched the speedometer to make sure we didn't drift out of the jet stream, because it would have used a lot of fuel to burn our way back in.

So we had to fight to keep ourselves awake, but, I think, being an entrepreneur and having to fight for my business life a lot, I don't give up easily. I'm also not somebody who dwells on things going wrong, or who gets downhearted. I enjoy life so much, I was just completely and utterly determined to survive this problem. Per, who is Swedish, was brought up to be tough, and he wasn't throwing in the towel either.

I flew the balloon for the next fifteen hours. At one moment I looked up at the big glass dome on the top of the capsule and suddenly imagined that these big cups of ice had caught fire and were raining down on top of the capsule. Because I was really, really tired I thought I might be seeing things, so I blinked a number of times, but then realised this was truly happening, and that if one of those balls of burning propane had hit the capsule top it would have shattered the glass and been the end of us. I shouted to Per, who had gone to sleep, to tell him what was happening. He snapped awake in seconds, and shouted '*Burn, burn, burn,*' at me, meaning I should open the burners to get higher, the aim being that the air would be thinner the higher we went and, hopefully, that would put the fire out ... although on the other hand the capsule was only pressurised to forty-two thousand feet.

Anyway, we got up to forty-two thousand feet and the fire was still not out so we had to take a risk and go up to forty-three, forty-four, forty-five thousand feet, which in itself could have broken the dome, but the extra pressure finally put the fire out, which was a huge relief.

During the next twenty-four hours we had no communications. We had lost all contact, which must have been worrying for everybody back home. But the speed continued, and then about eight hundred miles from the coast the radio crackled back on again and we were able to talk to base. They were particularly relieved to talk to us at that moment because they wanted to tell us that the jet stream had turned, and at the height we were going we were about to head back to Japan, but if we dropped from thirty-five thousand feet to ten thousand we might find some air that would take us up to the nearest land, which was towards the Arctic. Bob Rice, a meteorologist with the US National Weather Service, is a brilliant weatherman and we followed his instructions, going down to ten thousand feet, where we found a northerly – it's very rare to get them.

The wind swept us up north, then we were crossing land and had mountains below, although visibility was poor as we were coming into a heavy snowstorm. I climbed on to the top of the capsule to see if I could see a gap in the trees where we could land and, while I was out there, pulled out the safety bolts on the explosive bolts so we could release the balloon from the capsule when we landed. It was quite an eerie feeling sitting on the top of the capsule in a snowstorm, looking out through a forest of millions and millions of conifer trees. But I finally saw a lake up ahead and jumped back into the balloon.

Per was the more experienced pilot so he was flying the landing. I buckled myself in and braced myself. I fired the explosive bolts, which fortunately worked, and the balloon pulled off into the air – and got snagged on the trees ahead – then we crashed onto this icy lake, skidded along on top of it and came to a grinding halt. The only thing that saw us land was an otter, which walked across to inspect this new arrival, gave us a suspicious sniff and waddled off.

We walked out briefly, but it was minus 60 degrees and we'd taken clothes for a Los Angeles landing, not an Arctic one, so we very quickly got back into the capsule and literally huddled up together. I sent out an emergency signal and talked to somebody who asked, 'Richard, where are you?' I said, 'Well, we're on a lake, surrounded by trees,' to which he replied, 'There are something like half a million lakes in the area,' so I wasn't being very helpful. But fortunately they had seen our emergency-beacon signal and sent out helicopters from Yellowknife to rescue us, and they managed to get us out that night. We were on that lake about fifteen hours, I'd say. That lake didn't actually have a name, but I understand it's now called Lake Virgin.

We landed in Yellowknife early the following morning. All our friends and family had managed to get together and were there to greet us, which was wonderful.

Despite the sheer terror of it all it was a fantastic journey, and we achieved what we set out to do: we crossed the Pacific in a hot-air balloon, proving it could be done.

It's strange because some of the happiest days of my life have been on the adventure side of my life, trying to achieve new things that haven't been achieved before, and yet in the process of that there have been moments which have been sheer terror. But, having survived them, I've got lots of great stories to tell any grandchildren.

We were incredibly lucky to have survived that ditching, and I'm extremely appreciative to be alive. We should have obviously given up ballooning, but then we thought we'd have another adventure and try to go round the world, but that's another story.

PETER DONALDSON

I made a navigational error...

In 1939 I went up for an interview for a short service commission, but it was a ludicrous interview; some of the questions they asked me were absolutely impossible.

'Do you masturbate?'

Well, I didn't even know what that meant!

'What does your father do?'

I could have told a lie and said he was a bank manager, but he wasn't, he was a fish merchant, and as soon as you mentioned the words 'fish' and 'merchant' you didn't get a commission. But they offered me a job as under training observer, which is a navigator, and I accepted that, and was posted to 10 Squadron after my training and eventually started as a navigator.

10 Squadron was a member of Bomber Command, and it was our job to go on bombing raids over Germany, which we did. We flew the Whitley Mk V. They were all right to fly. Inadvertently,

they had one advantage that saved us: because they were very slow, German fighters couldn't believe we were going so slowly, and could not work out how to get at us, and I used to sit at my navigation table and see their tracer bullets going yards ahead of the nose of the plane. I don't remember being nervous – maybe I should have been – but I always had a feeling I was going to survive.

I did my first bombing raid on 20 April 1940. The target was Stavanger in Norway – the Germans had occupied Norway and were using it as one of their bases for their bombing activities. Sometimes, as well as navigating, I was doing the bombing myself, going into the front turret, looking through a bombsight and dropping the bombs. The Whitley carried five-hundred-pound bombs, but Stavanger airbase was built on solid rock and the thought occurred to us that whatever we dropped down there wasn't going to have much effect.

We were stationed at Dishforth in Yorkshire, and we took off one day – I can't now remember what the target was – and as we came over the sea we entered an extremely dynamic magnetic storm; there were flashes of lightning going between the guns in the rear turret, and, unknown to us, it caused the compass to go 180 degrees out. So we finished up going 180 degrees in the wrong direction, and I dropped a stick of bombs on what we thought was the runway of a German airbase – but it was Bassingbourn in Cambridgeshire. When the Air Ministry came to look at the result of that bombing, they couldn't believe the craters were so small, and realised we were using First World War bombs, which were completely ineffective. So a good thing came out of that fiasco in that we stopped using these old bombs.

All in all, I did eighteen night ops and two daylight raids, and so 8 July 1940 was going to be my twenty-first op. We took off at 2100 hours. The target was Kiel, but I made a navigational error and we flew in an easterly direction for longer than we should. I eventually realised my mistake, so we came back on the opposite course, but we were running short of fuel.

The captain of our plane was a chap called Flying Officer French-Mullins, who was a fantastic bloke. He said, 'I don't think we're going to make it, so I'm giving the order now that every-one prepare to ditch.' We hadn't yet dropped our bombs, so we dropped them right away into the sea.

When you're coming down on water, if the nose of your air-craft is too low you go right down, and if it's too high you pancake, and probably break the tail of the aircraft, so we had to get it absolutely right. But French-Mullins was a fantastic pilot and he made a perfect landing, and as soon as we ditched I opened the main exit door and threw out the dinghy.

We all got out of the aircraft and were floundering around in the water trying to right the dinghy, except French-Mullins, who used the escape hatch near his piloting position. He got on to the wing of the aircraft and stood there for a little while. 'Donaldson,' he said, 'would you mind moving the dinghy a little closer to where I am?' So I managed to push the dinghy towards him, and he just stepped into the dinghy off the wing. Oh, he was cool as a cucumber, was French-Mullins.

Eventually, all five of us got into the dinghy, and we were all very cold and wet through, and feeling a bit miserable – all, that is, except French-Mullins, he was the only one who was dry. 'Anyone want a cigarette?' he asked, and handed them round, and we all had a cigarette and watched the Whitley gradually sink beneath the waves.

After a while, French-Mullins said to me, 'Send up a distress flare, Donaldson, will you?' In the dinghy was our Very pistol, a flare gun, which sends a shot out into space, and so we sent one up, which could be seen from miles away, and very soon we heard a boat chugging towards us; in fact there were two fishing boats full of Germans, and French-Mullins and Carr, who was the second pilot, got into one boat, and we non-commissioned officers got into the other.

The German fishermen on my boat were some of the biggest chaps I've ever seen; their captain had these massive shoulders and he hauled me and the other NCOs aboard, and I felt very grateful to them because they saved our lives.

We had to go through a minefield to get to Heligoland, this German port they were taking us to, and one of the fishing boat's crew stood in the bow, pushing these mines apart with a long stick, which gave me a little bit of a tremble, I can tell you. But he obviously knew what he was doing, because we finally got to Heligoland, and we were taken to the German barracks, which had been hewn out of red rock; it was a bit like something out of a James Bond film. We were given dry clothes, and I finished up in a French uniform of some sort, and then we were put on a ferry, which operated between Heligoland and the mainland, and from there the five of us were taken by train to Frankfurt by German guards.

As we were being marched out of the station, heading for a prison camp, five of us in a straight line, with the guards front and back, I remember some of the men sweeping the road gave the

Hitler salute as we came past. Also, a man emerged from the crowd watching us. He actually cut right across in front of me, and said, in clear, perfect English, 'Don't worry, mate, you'll be all right ...'

We finished the journey in a German Army vehicle. The five of us comforted each other, but actually I was concerned about where we were heading, and what was going to happen to us. I knew a bit of German, and I asked one German guard, 'How do you treat prisoners in Germany?' And he replied, 'We are a civilised nation.' He obviously didn't know about Belsen.

Actually, the guards were all right, I have no complaints about them. We'd been given some German black bread, which I couldn't stomach, and one guard said to me, 'Why don't you eat your bread?' I replied, 'I don't like it', and seemed quite concerned, he said, 'You'd better eat it, you're going to go hungry otherwise.'

We eventually got to Stalag Luft, which was a reception camp for recently captured prisoners, and interrogated for about a week. They wanted to know the name of our commanding officer and squadron, and where it was situated and so on, but, of course, we just said, 'We are only able to give you our name, rank and number, nothing else ...' which is what I kept repeating. I can still remember my number, 580770: I'm sure they must have been thrilled with that information. The only thing I found difficult was that they wouldn't let us sleep; every time we dozed off, someone came in and woke us up, so we were suffering from sleep deprivation, which is a form of torture, in a sense. I suppose they felt we'd be more pliable to deal with if we were in that state of mind.

When they realised they couldn't get any further with us, we were transferred to Stalag Luft III prison camp. I remember we passed through a gate, and over the top of the gate was a message in German, *Arbeit Macht Frei*, Work Sets You Free, which is a load of rubbish. There were quite a lot of prisoners already there. I remember one chap called 'Horizontal' Jones, 'Horizontal' because he was always lying on his back half asleep. He was the first from the RAF to have been captured, so he was a bit of a celebrity, but he was also a very nice person.

Eventually, we were evacuated from there, and moved to Stalag Luft I in Barth, which is a nice little place on the Baltic coast.

Well, the whole time I was a prisoner I had escape on my mind. As a sergeant, I was not forced to work, but I volunteered to work – and made myself very unpopular with my comrades because they thought I was helping the Germans. But I reckoned that was my only opportunity for escape. I asked a friend of mine, Harry Stamford, to come along with me. Harry and I got on very well together; we never quarrelled, or argued, we were tremendous friends.

We were working in a coke factory, shovelling coke into a crushing machine, and every day I wore a greatcoat down to my knees, and I stuffed the pockets full of food and compasses and wire cutters, anything that could be useful for an escape, and they never searched me, which was fortunate. One day we walked down to the coke-crushing-machine area, and there were two or three guards mooching about. I said to the guard, 'I want to go to the toilet . . .' and when I got there Harry was trying to get out through a window, but was stuck. So I dragged him back in again, turned the handle of the door on the other side of the cubicle, which he hadn't tried, and it opened on to a little lane.

So we took this path, which went past a field of corn, and rested for a while near a haystack, while Messerschmitts were coming in over our heads, and landing at the airport just a mile away. I said, 'I don't think it's a very good idea to stay here, we might be spotted', and so we walked on further, and crossed a railway line. On reflection, we should have laid low there, and waited for a goods train to come along, and jumped into a wagon – I knew someone who did that and he got back home. But we didn't do that, we carried along the road. It was deserted to start with, and eventually we came to a little village ahead of us, and I can remember some German boys and girls playing with a hoop as we walked through. 'Should we continue to walk along the path, or dive into a forest on our right?' Harry asked. 'Oh, let's walk along, we'll be all right,' I said. That was a big mistake.

As we continued, we saw ahead of us a German policeman coming out of a little country police station. He put his hands on the handlebar of his bicycle, and his leg started to swing over to mount the bicycle, and then he saw us and his leg came down. He stayed like that, and when we finally got level with him, he pulled out his revolver, and I remember thinking, He's aiming that thing right between my eyes . . . So I put my hands up, we both did, and he marched us into the police station. He probably had a pretty good idea where we'd come from, because our prison camp was only a few miles away. I remember there was a great big picture of Hitler looking down on us from the wall. I also remember the policeman's daughter came in; she was about my age, eighteen, and she looked at us with great sympathy – that kind of immediate rapport between teenagers. Anyway, he picked up the telephone to call our prison camp, and he said, '*Heil Hitler*' over the telephone and saluted at the same time, which seemed absolutely ludicrous.

They came for us from the camp, so we were back in prison again, and they also put us in solitary confinement, and we were on bread and water for three weeks, which was a bit awful. France had been overrun by the Germans by that time, so they were using Frenchmen to guard us and these blighters were pinching our bread rations, which was all we had to live on, which was disgusting, wasn't it? That gave me a little bit of a prejudice against the French, I'm afraid to say; it shouldn't have, but it has. Anyway, we got by, and eventually we came out of solitary confinement, but I was so weak I had a job climbing into my bunk. Fortunately, a Red Cross food parcel came a few weeks later and helped me on a bit, particularly the chocolate, which gave me some energy.

I was a prisoner for nearly five years. The way people react in those circumstances is vastly different. Some people say, 'I'm going to try and escape, I'm not going to stay in this place any longer than I have to,' and others say, 'I'm not going to escape because I might get killed.' And some behave in a most outlandish way. I can remember one man who literally dressed himself up as a woman, and put lipstick on, and he sat like that all day, which was absolutely disgusting. I don't quite know what to say about that really.

The years passed by. Thanks to the Red Cross, we had a little library in our prison camp, so we had books to read, and I read a lot; also, I was given tuition by someone who had been a lecturer in mathematics before he'd joined up, and he taught me a lot about geometry and trigonometry.

We had a secret wireless which we'd made in our prison camp, by bribing guards with cigarettes in exchange for various parts, and we picked up that the British had invaded and were coming at some speed across Europe towards Germany. The Germans thought the best thing they could do with us was to round us all up and force-march us further into Germany. No doubt the idea was to use us as hostages. So we were put on this forced march towards the Baltic coast. I was walking along with an Irishman called Paddy Dixon. We came to this road that curved around, and realised that for a few seconds the guard in the front and the guard behind wouldn't be able to see us, so we made a dash for it, and got completely away, into this forest near Hallam, to the east of Hanover.

We had no compass and no food, and we were getting hungry and thirsty, but eventually we saw a small rise going up into the forest. So we climbed this hill, and all around us were Russians, who'd been prisoners of war and had escaped.

The Russians had survived by taking food from German farmers. On our first night with them, someone said to me, 'We're going to put you down a chute into this potato store: fill up a sack of potatoes and we'll then pull you out.' Oh, thanks very much, I thought. But that worked like a treat, and for the next few weeks we would go to a different farmhouse, and, while the farmer and his wife were asleep in bed, we'd take their food and animals. I stayed with these Russians in their little hideout for several weeks and we lived like lords. Each night we ate something different: we had roast duck, we had roast chicken, you mention it, we had anything we wanted. In fact, when I got back to England shortly after the war, I was standing in a line with other POWs, waiting to be examined by a medical officer, and all I could hear in front of me was '*You've* got malnutrition,' '*You've* got malnutrition . . .' Then they came to me. 'Hey, where have you been?'

I became very fond of those Russians, they were incredible blokes, really marvellous people, and became great pals. When the area was finally overrun by the British 10th Armoured Division, and it was time for me to leave, they all came to see me off, some of them on a horse and cart they'd pinched from a German farmer. And, a few days later, we were evacuated and came back home and that was the end of my captivity.

It had been a very dangerous situation for a long, long time. For example, after we escaped, we could have been shot. I had a great friend who'd escaped from prison camp and got into Poland, and lived with a woman for some months, but he was betrayed to the Germans, and when they recaptured him he was put up against a brick wall and shot. A picture was taken of his body lying in a pool of blood, and this picture was brought to our prison camp to show prisoners what happens to people who try to escape. But I am glad I had these adventures; well, life would have been a bit boring without them, and when you're young you put up with discomforts, starvation, or whatever it may be. Also, whatever happened to me in later life was nothing after what I'd been through in the war.

I hold no resentment towards the Germans. I've met some extremely pleasant and kind Germans, even when I was a prisoner. I made friends with a guard at one prison camp; he spoke good English, and I had a leather-bound copy of Longfellow's poems and offered it to him, and he wouldn't take it. He said,

'I've been transferred to an anti-aircraft gun on the coast, and I can't be firing at your comrades and accept this book.' I don't think the French would have behaved like that.

I stayed in the RAF for a while after the war – I wasn't quite sure what I wanted to do with my life, and needed some time to think about it. I decided to retrain as a teacher, and spent the next thirty years teaching. I was headmaster of a school in Chorleywood, and head of a small country school in the Yorkshire Dales. I enjoyed my work as a teacher enormously, it really made my life meaningful. I still go to reunions of schools where I was headmaster; they invite me around, although most of my pupils are in their forties and fifties now.

I've had an enormous amount of love in my life; I have made some amazing friendships, and I am still loved by my children and friends. But I'm ninety in a month's time. My wife died five years ago; we were married for sixty years and I loved her to bits. She was the most beautiful, lovable woman. I can't describe to you how much I loved her, and how much I miss her, and what I really want to do now is to die. I really want to die, because I believe I'll be reunited with her. And I'm not afraid of death, as you can see. I've faced it many times in my life. Also, I'm old, and my memory's deteriorating, and I just feel now that I don't want to grow any older and finish up in a wheelchair being pushed about. So I want to get out of it now. It's rather like escaping from a prison camp in a way.

HARVEY HORN

Whoops, this could be dangerous . . .

I grew up in an area called Borough Park in Brooklyn, which was essentially a Jewish neighbourhood. I was a gung-ho kid, a real flag-waver: the FBI could do no wrong, the government was always right. Well, along came Pearl Harbor. I was listening to the Giants game on the radio, and they interrupted the game to flash, 'The Japanese have bombed Pearl Harbor.' I asked my folks, 'Where's that?', because I'd never heard of it, and then I decided I wanted to enlist; my reaction was, we had to defend our country, it was as simple as that.

So I went down to Church Street, and I passed the aptitude test, although 50 per cent of the people there failed. Mind you, if they tried that now, I guarantee 75 per cent would not be taken; I mean, we have a fat problem in our country that is unbelievable. I'm talking about obese. Then I called up my folks. 'Hey Mom, guess what? They accepted me.' There was a pause, a big pause, and finally she said, 'OK.'

For basic training we went to Atlantic City. Atlantic City felt like a real adventure. I had only been out of New York once, when I was sixteen; I went to the Catskills to visit a girlfriend. We stayed at the Traymore Hotel, which was an art deco type of hotel. We did callisthenics, and marched on the boardwalk – and we trained to the beat of Glenn Miller's band.

We had ten hours of Piper Cub flying in Burlington, Vermont, what they called pre-flight, and then they sent us down to Nashville for classification, and gave us all kinds of aptitude testing, and I qualified: pilot, navigator, bombardier. Max Field was where they really worked you over, and we did the Burma Road, which was the ultimate obstacle course, ten miles of hell, although I was so fit in those days I could sprint the last mile and not even feel it. For your information, I'm eighty-nine now, and I'm still a good athlete, and do a very credible job on the tennis court; it's not pat-a-cake.

After that, I went to gunnery school in Fort Myers, got my gunnery wings, then they shipped me down to the Pan American School of Navigation where we learned celestial navigation. You have to memorise sixty-four stars, but I would select three stars triangularly spaced to take bearings with my sextant. If you look at the three big stars in the northern hemisphere, Vega, Deneb and Altair, they always form a right triangle.

And then, finally, they sent us to Drew Field, Tampa, Florida, to meet the crew we'd be flying with, and we trained together. Captain John Lincoln, the pilot, came from California. He was twenty-seven, which seemed old to me as a nineteen-year-old. He was a good-looking fellow, very quiet I remember. The second oldest on the plane, and his first lieutenant, was Lorin Millard. Lorin was an Ohio farm boy, big, tall, strong, a very solid guy and a good pilot. George was twenty-eight, he came from Rochester, and the flight engineer was Evlyn Linnane, a big, red-headed Irish guy from Chicago. But I didn't hang out with those guys, I was closer to the crew, who were more my age. Herbert 'Smokey' Stover was the radio operator, Lou Brown and Herb Brown were the tail gunners, Herb Wagner was a waist gunner and Lou Michel was the ball turret gunner. And that was all ten of us.

When we were ready, we were sent to Savannah to pick up a B-17. *Pretty Baby's Boys* was the name of our plane. Up until that time I was having a ball, I'm living the dream, wow . . . But then it struck me: Whoops, this could be dangerous! Am I ever going to come back? But I didn't think about it too long.

We tested the plane, fired the machine guns and callipers and gave it a rough go. We had to break it in. We went out on missions at low and high levels, and we learned to fly with other groups in formation, and then we all took a shot at flying the plane in the right seat. The B-17, the Flying Fortress, is a fabulous plane. Maybe it flies a little slower than the B-24, but it goes much higher, and it takes unbelievable punishment, and it stays together in one piece when you crash it.

And then we were given sealed orders and we took off.

We first landed in Corning, in a big, huge snowstorm. Wow! I'd never seen such an amount of snow. But by the morning they got the runway cleared and we took off. The sun was out, it was one of those big, blue, open-sky days, and you could see everything clear as a bell, such a great feeling. After that we went to Gander, in Canada, which was bitch cold, and we were freezing our asses off, and I had to cover the engines to stop them icing up.

The next day we were supposed to take off at one o'clock, but we had some mechanical problems and didn't take off until evening, and headed off to the Azores. Flying at night, and over water, you cannot use dead reckoning, but I accurately predicted the ETA, zero/zero, and I was real proud.

From there we went to Marrakesh, which was hot, hot, hot, and dusty, and we had to cover the engines again, this time to protect them against the dust. John, George and Lorin went into the bazaar in Marrakesh, but I didn't go with them; I had no interest in looking around foreign places, I was such an immature twenty. They came back with a bottle of gin, and it was the first time I'd tried it, and I was very sick.

From there, we flew the plane over to Bari in Italy, and then they bussed us to Foggia, where we joined the 15th Air Force to bomb factories in Berlin, which was the longest mission ever flown by the 15th Air Force.

Berlin was very heavily fortified, and they had the 88 ack-ack, anti-aircraft guns, which were fantastic, best guns ever made, and all our planes were barely making it back. We only just made it, our whole plane was riddled with flak. I was sitting with my chest against the bombardier's back, and some time during the run he got hit by flak in the shoulder. So I cut open his jacket and put salt on the wound. It wasn't too deep and he coped OK, and, anyway, loss of blood at altitude is not too serious because everything's frozen. But as far as I know we hit the targets. It's a race to hit the IP, the initial point, and cut away or be hit, but you stay on the run because that's what you're there to do – you drop the bombs and off you go. A ten- to twelve-minute bombing run over targets like heavily fortified Berlin or Vienna were real sweat jobs: the bomber must keep air speed and altitude constant, so we were sitting ducks for the 88s.

Our next mission was to bomb the marshalling yards at Amstetten, Austria, south of Vienna. The only change from the last sortie was that we were going to be doing pattern bombing. Anything that could fly was up in the air, one thousand planes or more, and before we left I stood on the ground watching the planes go over: wave after wave after wave of B-17s, B-24s and B-25 fighter planes, flying in formation as far as the eyes could see. I was spellbound by that sight.

We took off about six o'clock, we came up over clouds, and then we started to form in groups and make our way up. We crossed the Adriatic, and began going over the Yugoslavian Alps, and then, over Zagreb, Lou Brown yelled, 'We're hitting flak,' and Herb reported the same thing a minute or two later, and a bit of shrapnel hit his hand.

Suddenly, the hydraulic system was shot and we lost number-three engine. I immediately checked to see what my options were. We were sixty miles away from the Adriatic Sea. Should we go to Switzerland? Russia? Or turn back to Italy and try to make it back to the Adriatic landing base? John was talking on the intercom to our group leader, and then he says to us, 'We're going to try and make it to the Adriatic, dump everything that's not nailed down.' And that's what we did. Everything went out, ammunition, bombs, maps, the guys even tried to unbuckle the ball gun, which they couldn't do.

Unfortunately we then lost our other engine. So we've got one engine smoking, two are shot, gone, and the Italians are now firing at us. We just made it over the Yugoslavian Alps, and we had a door open and were so low I could almost touch the snow. One wing was now up, but John and Lorin miraculously righted the plane, and we ditched near the city of Fiume, Italy, which is now Rijeka, Croatia, about six miles from the shore. We hit the water at ninety miles an hour. You get the shit kicked out of you at that speed, because you're bouncing forward and bouncing back, you're just like a rubber ball. And then finally it stopped, and the water came in.

But I'm proud of the crew, I really am; this was no sweat job, none of us had any moments of hysteria, no freezing, no fear, the crew went about the ditching process just as if we were in training.

Above me the hatch was open. The guys started to go up in

rotation, Lorin was standing by the ladder and I gave him a shove, and said, 'Get your ass up', or words to that effect, and then finally I went up, and I was the last one up from the plane.

We were all sitting up on the wing, soaking wet and cold. We released the two rubber boats, one inflated, the other we had to hand-inflate, and the five of us officers got into one boat and the crew into the other, and we started to paddle.

A grey-painted German gunboat motored out from Fiume Harbour, similar in size to an American Coast Guard river patrol boat. There were five or six sailors on board, with an officer in charge. Three or four sailors held machine guns on us as the boat came alongside. Their clothes were dark blue, and they had some Nazi insignias on their sleeves.

The officer told us to unbelt the Colt 45s we all carried, which were collected by a sailor. Two sailors tied a rope to the front of each of our dinghies and we were towed to shore.

None of us spoke during the short trip to the dock, but I remember I made a mental promise to myself to get a German Luger to replace my 45. I kept that promise.

They marched us down this large, wide street, and it was like the circus had come to town and we're the animals. All the time people were shouting insults at us: 'Lower than dirt', 'Bastards', things like that. Other people just stared at us, open-mouthed. They couldn't forget we Allies had bombed their city time and time again.

We were marched to what I found out many years later was St Peter's Church. Behind the church was this manor house with wooden gates and high walls, and they stood us in front of this pockmarked grey wall, and there's a German guy with a machine gun in front of each one of us. Holy shit, they're going to shoot us, and that's when fear takes over.

But after about twenty minutes, they motioned to us to march into the manor house, and they gave us ersatz coffee, which is crappy coffee that just goes right through you, black bread and cabbage soup. And then they started to interrogate us: 'Name, rank and serial number.' After they did that they left us alone, and we went to sleep on the table where we were all seated at benches.

The next morning they marched us out with a group of soldiers to a tramcar full of Italian civilians going to work. I remember standing on the strap with a guard next to me, and there was this one good-looking Italian girl, a brunette, about seventeen or eighteen. Man, oh man, she was really built. The sun was coming in through the window, and she didn't have a bra on, and I could see the shape of her boobs, and I kept thinking about that, although I also thought, What the hell's wrong with you, guy? You shouldn't be having that kind of stuff on your mind now ...

They took us to Trieste, and there they put us in an SS prison and separated us; the five officers were put in one cell and the five crew in another. They then started interrogation. John went first. He was out for a couple of hours. He came back and said, 'They know everything about us, they know my full middle name, my parents' name and address, all they wanted was confirmation.' Lorin went out next, and came back a couple of hours later too.

And then I went out. But I didn't go into the interrogation room; they put me in this small cell, about three by nine, and locked the door. It was pitch black, so I started feeling all over the walls: there's got to be something I can grab on which will open sesame – it works in the movies, baby. But that didn't work and I started thinking, I know why I'm here, it's because I'm a Jew ... And, being Jewish, with the Germans, that's not a good scene, and I really got frightened then. I can't express the anxiety and fear of being a Jew and a POW. I started to think about my parents, and how they might never know what happened to me.

And then I thought about my dog tag, which I was wearing. All American servicemen wore one of three dog tags, P, C or H, which stood for Protestant, Catholic or Hebrew. I had an H dog tag on. I thought, OK they're going to know for sure with the H that I'm Jewish. Shall I keep it on?

I agonised over that one. Should I throw it away or keep it on? I thought about being Jewish, and what it means to me, and then I realised: Fuck 'em, I'm going to keep it on. In that cell I decided you have to acknowledge who you are in life, it's important. I was H. At that point I was ready to take on the Germans. Not a brave thing to do. It was stupid. I should have thrown it away, although my friend Marty Bell, who's passed away now, told me he threw his dog tag away and had guilt feelings about that for ever.

But once I made the decision I would keep on the dog tag, I lay down on the cold cement floor and actually fell asleep. I don't know how long I slept – it could have been one day, it could have been two – but eventually they opened the door.

These guys took me to an office down the hallway. They opened the door, and sitting behind a desk was an SS captain in a black uniform. He didn't look at me. One guard said, 'Sit down,' and I sat down. Finally, the SS man looked up from his papers. 'What's your name, rank, serial number?' He tells me the other guys have told him such and such, which I didn't believe. And then he comes to the question about my being Jewish. 'Yeah,' I said, 'I'm Jewish,' showing him my dog tag, 'what about it?' 'American Jews are OK,' he said, 'it's European Jews we don't like,' and he talked a bit about that. And then eventually he sent me back to the other guys, and after that I wasn't treated any differently from them.

We stayed in that prison for five or six days, but all I remember about that place now was the lice and the boredom.

After that, we went to Oudenay and we stayed there a couple of days, and from there they took us to Verona and we had to walk. We had to walk for days. I was wearing my flying slippers from our plane, as I'd taken off my boots when we had ditched, and my feet were in terrible shape, blisters and everything.

We stayed in Verona for a while, and we ate fairly well there; we had the same food as the Luftwaffe. There's a lot of stories about the Luftwaffe treating Allied airmen with respect and concern, which goes back to the First World War. Then we marched up through the Brenner Pass into Austria and Germany, which was a pretty long march, and, on top of that, they gave each of us a fifty-pound bag of grain to carry for the German soldiers. My feet were so blistered up by that time I could barely walk, and I was in agony. Somebody found me a pair of boots, but I didn't have enough time to heal, so they were no help. We were on the road for days, and finally I just stopped. 'I can't walk any more,' I said.

So I'm lying down on the ground, and a German pokes me

with his rifle butt: '*Raus, raus*,' he says, and then this Frenchman says to him, 'He can't move, shoot him ...' And you know something? I was hurting so much I didn't care. But I tell you: the French are a group of people who are out of step with so many other people, even now.

Anyway, eventually we got to Munich, which was practically destroyed. We marched through the streets, and we could see building after building partially or completely destroyed, and bricks and rubble in the streets. The next day they separated us: the officers went to Nuremberg and the enlisted men went to Mossberg.

Nuremberg was under siege, the Third Army was coming down south, and they were in a hurry to get down south to Munich, because they thought they could catch Hitler. So we were being shelled by the US forces, and the repercussions from the shells were shaking the town like crazy. We had been herded into a farmhouse, and we got a white sheet and stuck it on a broom, and waved it. The 86th Black Hawk [Infantry] Division guys took us to a castle in the town, which was the American HQ, and we stayed there for a few days while they checked us out and confirmed we were Americans, because sometimes the Germans would get US uniforms and impersonate us.

After we got the OK, we were given commanding general orders to go to Paris. We flew into Paris on a C-47, in one of the worst storms I'd ever been in. 'Gee John,' I said, 'I wish you were flying this thing.' We were put up in a hotel, and in the evening we went to the Folies Bergère, and a couple of us went out afterwards to dinner some place and we met some French girls. I no longer remember exactly what happened that night, but I didn't score, I can tell you that.

We were then ordered to go to London. We took a boat from Dieppe, and as we approached Dover we could see the white cliffs. They trucked us to London and put us up in a hotel. London was bombed pretty badly, and we were bombed while we there, and had to go across the street to the bomb shelter in the underground. When we got there, Londoners were reading their books, or playing cards, some were sleeping, it was all very casual and orderly. Everyone waited for the All Clear, and when it came we went upstairs.

We were given orders to go to Southampton and get on the last official convoy. The ship was crowded with ex-POWs, and lots of injured. The ship was all blacked out, because we weren't sure all the U-boats had got word the war was over. But on the last night, the black drapes were removed, lights went on all over the place, oh, it was quite a sight, and they brought up anyone who could be brought up, who wasn't locked into beds. The captain deliberately came up the New York Bay very slowly, and everyone was shouting and cheering, waving their arms, just carrying on. 'We're going home!' But, suddenly, as we got to the Statue of Liberty, there was a deathly silence, you could hear a pin drop, and as we looked at the Statue of Liberty everyone was thinking, We made it, we're alive, oh wow. It was very emotional.

They then trucked us to Atlantic City. The song I marched to on the Atlantic City boardwalk was the 'St Louis Blues', played swing style à la Glenn Miller. When I take my constitutional walks I still hum that song. Some things stay with you.

We were then given sixty days' leave, and I went home. My folks didn't know I was coming home, and my mother was all emotional and teary eyed. But I didn't tell them about my war, in fact I didn't speak about it for fifty-five years, until I wrote a story for my great-niece's school project. And then I started talking. Now I talk a lot about it, particularly how you shouldn't wage war unless you really have to.

After the war I went to engineering school and had a successful career in plastics. I met and married a very difficult, unhappy individual and it was a complete disaster. But she was a crutch: I needed someone to help me perform, act, go back to school, get a job, and she was there at the time. Certain things were bothering me, certain things that were a direct result of my experience, and when I was about sixty I started getting anxiety attacks so severe that I couldn't function. This is not abnormal with prisoners of war – years pass, and, all of a sudden, something triggers. Now I'm in a group and doing therapy with POW guys every week, and I've learned a lot about myself from the psychologists, and about the things that happened.

I can tell you what it comes down to in simple terms. How come I am here today and other guys are not? Why did I survive? I'm ashamed to say I only did two missions, and I was only a POW for thirty-six days. What's the big deal? I didn't do enough, and I wasn't captured long enough. It bothers me that I got off so lightly. Guys were doing twenty-five missions, fifty missions. There's a guy I play tennis with who was in the Hanoi Hilton⋆ for six years. And another part of it is that I was captured: there's shame attached to that.

⋆The American nickname for the place where the North Vietnamese incarcerated US pilots who had been shot down during the Vietnam War.

Anyway, I don't feel that now. Now I feel proud that I did what I thought was the right thing to do by enlisting, and I did what was asked of me at a time of urgency, because my country needed my participation. I served my country, and I did the best I could, and I put my life on the line. And I'm alive, I'm here.

Fortunately, I got lucky. I married a most marvellous person the second time around, and this January it will be forty-six years, and it's been a ball . . . Thank God for Minerva, she's a wonderful person, and calms me down.

At this stage of the game I've lost a lot of friends. Lorin Millard, our co-pilot, just turned ninety-three. I decided I wanted to see him while he's still pretty good, because he has throat cancer, and has stopped radiation, because it's not going to make much difference. I wanted to thank him, and to feel the relationship one last time, and say goodbye without saying goodbye, if you know what I mean.

So, a couple of weeks ago I flew out to see him; he's living with his daughter in Youngstown, Ohio. The first thing he said to me was, 'I've shrunk . . . ' I remember what he looked like all those years ago – a big, strapping farm boy – and when I saw him now he looked like a ninety-three-year-old: stooped, and he had lost weight, thirty-five pounds at least, although of course I didn't blink an eye.

I asked him: 'Lorin, how in the hell were you and John able to fly the B-17 over the Yugoslavian Alps on one engine? It's an unbelievable feat, you guys saved all our lives.' And we talked about what we went through, and about our lives. I said I'd be back, and I will be, for his funeral. I want to do that for him.

POWs have a ceremony; we stand up and face the casket, we give a slow salute and we then turn around and read the 23rd Psalm.

Finally, we turn around and salute one last time. I hope they'll do the same for me.

The Lord is my shepherd; I shall not want.
He makes me lie down in green pastures,
He leads me beside quiet waters,
He restores my soul.
He guides me in paths of righteousness
For His name's sake.
Even though I walk through the valley of the shadow of death,
I will fear no evil
For you are with me;
Your rod and staff they comfort me.

ANDREW MOSELEY

'Even the bloody seagulls will be walking . . . '

With a name like Moseley we were assumed to have Fascist sympathies; we had some difficulty explaining that we were a totally different family, with two 'e's in our name, rather than Sir Oswald Mosley, whose actions were rife in the East End at that time. So the locals murmured among themselves, and at one stage even accused my mother of having defective blackout to attract the Germans.

My brother and I were madly patriotic, and we wondered what we could do to join the war effort, even though we were very young at the beginning of the war. I joined the LDV, the Local Defence Volunteers, which was the predecessor of the Home Guard. Our duty was to cycle from Braunton to Saunton Sands, near where we lived in Devon, and then sit 'on watch' in the bar of the hotel. That's where I was introduced to drinking beer. All we had to defend Saunton Sands were these ancient shotguns plus a First World War machine gun mounted prominently at the top of the cliff. We had a wizened, retired First World War sergeant in charge of us, and on one occasion I asked him, 'What's the use of a machine gun without any ammunition?' 'Well,' he said, 'if the Jerries come, we'll throw it at the buggers.'

We sat in there night after night, and after a bit I got a bit fed up. I couldn't wait to do something proper in the war. I went to the selection centre in Bristol, and probably because of my shorter stature I was chosen to be an observer/navigator rather than a pilot, which disappointed me, but never mind.

Then it was on to Whale Island for what they called gunnery training, which was square bashing and manning guns, subsequently to Eastleigh for radio/wireless training and Morse code, and then we were sent out one dark night to Scotland with our hammocks and kitbags, where we boarded the *Queen Elizabeth*, and sailed over to America. There were about five thousand troops on board and they had bunks stacked five high.

We arrived in New York on the last Thursday of November.

Now, can you imagine leaving bombed, rationed UK, and hitting New York on Thanksgiving Day?

The petty officer stood us in line, and said, 'Listen here, men. This is what they call Thanksgiving Day in the United States of America, and we have very kindly been invited to five Thanksgiving Day lunches. I want you to eat as much at the last one as you do at the first.' So it was turkey, cranberry sauce, the whole works, five times, and then we came back and recovered.

Later that night we were taken to the Stork Club. That was quite amazing, such a glamorous location with all these dancing girls, and they fed us champagne. The *Daily News* took a picture of one of our number, who had broken a leg when he slipped on the crossing on the *Queen Elizabeth*, with a showgirl on his knee. And the newspaper appeared on the news-stands the following morning with the headline 'British War Hero Hits New York!'

We then made our way to Trinidad to do flight training. The previous course sent to Trinidad had been torpedoed by a German submarine en route, so we didn't sail from New York; we went up to Providence on Rhode Island, and were then loaded on to an American troopship. We arrived in time for Christmas. Trinidad was amazing, because we had excellent food, we could go ashore, and we went into the capital, Port of Spain, where you drank rum and Coca-Cola and you could go to beaches nearby on a bus.

We had a theatre in the mess, and on one occasion Noël Coward came and entertained us. He sang 'Mad Dogs and Englishmen' and 'I Went to a Marvellous Party', and he was just as you might imagine him, suave, very well groomed in a tropical-type jacket and trousers, and camp as Christmas. The sailors loved it.

There were constant reports of losses of ships to torpedoes, particularly in the north Caribbean, so we joined a huge convoy coming across the Atlantic back to the UK. There was air cover as we left New York, but not in the middle of the Atlantic, which, of course, was where the U-boats loved to operate. We suffered the loss of several ships in the convoys. I actually saw at least two disappear: you wanted to do something to help, but what could we do? I felt totally helpless, angry and depressed.

Eventually, we landed in Portsmouth, and then after a spell of leave we went to the Royal Naval College at Greenwich, where they tried to turn us into gentlemen. That was a weird situation; we were eating in the Painted Hall with Wrens wearing gloves serving us, and in the meantime there were buzz bombs over-head. We were also learning unarmed combat there; I can remember one old bloke, who would teach us the falls and how

to strangle a sentry, and all these sort of things. I can remember his pep talks: 'You lot are going to end up in the Pacific, and you are going to face the Japanese. Don't trust the buggers,' he said. 'If you've lost your weapon, whip off your tin hat and cut his bloody head off with the end of it.' It was ruthless stuff.

I was then sent again to New York, resplendent in my uniform, and we were put into the Barbizon Plaza Hotel, the height of luxury, where we were introduced at cocktail parties to very attractive young ladies. It has since transpired they were put there by a character called Ironside, who was in charge of British Intelligence in America during the Second World War, to make sure we didn't do anything untoward. I had an extremely attractive girl who I could go dancing with, and on one occasion she even invited me to her home on Long Island. I thought, Great, you're in here. But when we arrived I was shown a separate bedroom. I wandered down in the morning and I saw two meaty fists holding up the *New York Times*, so I gave a discreet cough, and down it went, and there was this fierce-looking man, who said, 'In God's name, who are you?' That was her father.

We then went up to a US naval airbase in Lewiston, Maine, where we did our first deck landings. The night before we were due to fly, the met officer had told us, 'No flying tomorrow, even the bloody seagulls will be walking.' So we went out and got ourselves well oiled on beer. Bright and early the following morning, a steward came and gave us a shake. 'You're flying in half an hour,' he said. My pilot was giggling so much he had to be helped into the cockpit, and I was in the back feeling no pain either. Anyway, our pilot made his first deck landing that morning, and he did the most brilliant landing I have ever seen. .

I came back again on leave, and then we were sent up to an airfield near Blackpool where we did day and night torpedo-dropping attacks in the North Sea. Then we were told we were going out to Ceylon, as it was then called. We were stationed in the naval air station there, which was a 700 Squadron, designed to provide replacements for topping up the Fleet, although we did a few anti-submarine patrols over the Pacific for a couple of months. Then HMS *Implacable* came through and we were sent on board as a replacement crew. Eventually we started working up for the assault on Truk, which was a little island off Okinawa, still controlled by the Japanese.

The American invasion fleet was gathering offshore. Then, on about the second night, all the planes were lined up on the deck of the carrier, and the torpedo planes were at the front of the ship. The first plane was shot off on a catapult, and the next one had very little deck or space on which to go. Behind them were the Corsairs, American fighters, and Seafires. Seafires were at the stern of the ship, so they had the maximum amount of area for take-off. On this one dark night a good friend of ours was the first off the catapult; the catapult misfired and instead of taking him off it chucked the plane over the side of the ship, although I didn't know at the time, because we were getting ready to be the third off.

The third plane off is really short of space, and our engine failed on take-off and the plane went straight into the water. The pilot and the gunner managed to get out, but my canopy wouldn't open. I was trapped in this thing and I had the experience of hearing the ship going over the top of me. I even heard the propellers whirling around.

There was a release mechanism on the side, and I was tugging away at this lever, trying to get this bloody canopy off, but it was stuck. I had an oxygen mask, of course, but that wasn't functioning, so there must have been a little bubble of air in the canopy, which sustained me, but for two hours, while I was wrestling with this lever, I was worrying that each breath would be my last.

Eventually, the canopy broke away and, more dead than alive, with the aid of my Mae West I bobbed up to the surface in the dark, until I was picked up by a rear-screen destroyer called *Terpsichore*.

They launched a whaler from the ship to pick me up. The only thing I remember was being brought over the side, and vomiting all over the place, and thinking to myself, my God they will kill me for making a mess of their ship. I was taken down to the sickbay and I must have been anaesthetised or something because I fell asleep immediately. The sickbay attendant said to me the following morning as I came to, 'You aren't half lucky, sir, the doc on board is a pathologist in Civvy Street, and he was longing to get his hands on you!'

I was then transferred on a stretcher to a Dutch hospital ship, which was alongside, and from there I was taken to Manaus and transferred to a naval hospital. I was only there two nights, and then was put on an ambulance plane and sent down to the Royal Naval hospital in Sydney, where I spent the rest of the war.

That accident probably saved my life, because friends of mine from the same squadron went on to the islands; several of them were shot down, some were beheaded by the Japanese and others were taken prisoners of war. The loss of friends seems unreal somehow. The brutal reality doesn't impact on you right away;

it's almost as though they have disappeared over the horizon – maybe they have been posted somewhere else?

I did dream about my ditching for a long time afterwards. And I forced myself to swim, and to swim underwater, because for a long time I dreaded water. In fact, the first thing I did when I had a bit of money was to build a swimming pool, and I swim every morning of my life to overcome this terror of swimming underwater.

NORAH ANDERSON

I was such a polite girl . . .

I was eighteen when war broke out, and it became obvious I would be called up at some time, so I thought about which branch of the Services I would like to join and decided on the Wrens. I went for an interview, and the Wrens officer asked what

I wanted to do. My typing and shorthand skills were quite good, so I said I could be a secretary. 'Oh no, I don't want you for that,' she said. 'We have just opened a new category, and as you have had a good education and matriculated, we would like you to be a radio mechanic.'

I was quite shocked by that, because I had no idea about radio, or mechanics, and furthermore, my dream of being secretary to a dishy vice-admiral at the Admiralty had now been dashed. But in some way I felt I was fighting Hitler, because the officer explained they were bringing in women to be this category of mechanic in order to free a male radio mechanic, who would then be sent abroad to fight.

So that was that. I was duly called up, and had to report to Westfield College, Hampstead, where we had a month's probation in civvies. We learned how to speak naval speak. For instance, the kitchen was 'the galley', and had 'runs ashore', and if you were late you 'were adrift'. Later on, we learned things like how to salute an officer, bringing your right hand straight up to your eyebrow, and how the back of your hand should face the officer – hiding the sight of tar-stained palms is the historical explanation. We were in bunk beds, and each bed had a blue and white counterpane, the central motif of which was an anchor, and if by any chance you put that on the wrong way up, which meant sinking the ship, you were in real trouble.

I was meeting all kinds of new people. I was in one bunk with a girl who was also going to be a radio mechanic, and she became a friend, but there was a steward called Petal, who slept in the bunk next door, and I was quite shocked because she never removed her make-up.

After passing probation, we were finally kitted out with the Wrens uniform, the dark jacket and skirt, white shirt, black tie and a white hat with a little turned-up brim. That was a proud moment, and I felt I was the cat's whiskers when I went home on leave.

The first half of the course lasted very nearly eight months. There were sailors on the same course, though not in the same class, but in the break we would go up on to the roof and meet them there, which was fun. We were then posted to Lee-on-Solent, Hampshire, and we learned how to solder and wire things up safely, and we even made tools, and finally began to learn about the sets we would be using. I had been a Girl Guide, so I knew Morse code, but knowing it and tapping it out at great speed are two different things.

We had tests all the way along the line, and a big examination at the end, which I passed, and those who passed were upgraded from Wren to Leading Wren, which gave us a shilling or so more a week. Oh, I was very proud sewing on my new rank, which was a little blue anchor on the left arm, and the radio mechanic's signal on the right sleeve.

When the postings were allocated, I was hoping to go somewhere nice on the south coast, but as luck would have it the posting was to Arbroath in Scotland, which couldn't have been much further away from London. So off I went on the *Flying Scotsman* from King's Cross.

I worked on the Supermarine Walrus aircraft, and took the wireless set out of the plane into the workshop, and tested it there, and then would go into the aircraft to see that all the wiring had been done right. The Walrus was huge, and a rather strange and ugly looking plane in a way, with its engine and propeller at the back, not like some of the other planes I worked on, which looked athletic and sleek, like a Spitfire or a Hurricane.

One day I was told I would need to fly in the Walrus while it was being tested, which came as a bit of a surprise: I don't remember anybody else doing it. Anyway, I put on a life jacket and a parachute harness, plus flying helmet and flying boots, and everything felt very heavy climbing into the aircraft, I must say.

We took off, and I don't remember being told we were going to land on the sea, but it must have been part of the test, as the Walrus was amphibious, so it could land on the ground and on the water. We landed on the sea with a terrible judder, everything shook, and then it took off again, but almost immediately it nosedived into the sea. I fell forward and hit my head on the wireless set, and I was really badly bruised because we were flung about, and I must have been quite concussed too, because I can only remember some of what happened next.

I can remember the water absolutely gushing in, and panicking: dear God, how do we get out? And I don't know how I got out, but the next memory is of being in the water, which was very choppy, dark and menacing – and cold: it was the North Sea in February, after all – plus the added inconvenience of being weighed down with all these heavy things I was wearing.

I remember the pilot swimming towards me, and saying, 'Can you swim, Anderson?' 'Yes, thank you, sir,' I replied, 'can you?' I was such a polite girl; if I'd had my hat on I would have saluted him.

Next memory I have is being dragged out of the water by a boat hook, and put into a launch that had been sent by the RAF

HQ, and from there seeing our plane sinking in the distance. I remember lying in the launch and they cut my tie off, and I thought, Oh dear, I shall be in trouble for that! I also remember seeing a radio set up on a shelf, and thinking, That's an 1161, one of the wireless sets we worked on. I recognised it because it had a little green light that fluctuated with the signal coming in. I also remember being carried ashore and on to the harbour front, and hearing this lovely Scottish lady's voice saying, 'Och, it's a wee girl,' when she saw me being helped ashore.

I was taken to the RAF's station in Montrose and put in the sickbay, and caused quite a kerfuffle, didn't I, being the only female. They put me on bed rest, and I wasn't allowed to get up or do anything for nearly two weeks. However, the doctor looking after me was Flying Officer Nelson, and he was very, very kind, and I must say I was most disappointed when a naval ambulance turned up one day to take me back to Arbroath, because I was doing very nicely with Flying Officer Nelson.

From there I was sent home on sick leave, and, what's more, I was given a first-class ticket to go home to London, which was a real luxury. Generally, I went third class, and most of that was night travel, and packed with Armed Forces, so you would sit in a cramped seat, with a sailor resting his head on one shoulder and a soldier on the other.

Nothing was ever said or done about the accident, and no one ever interviewed me. I don't know whether it was the pilot's fault, or engine failure. I believe that the pilot was posted elsewhere quite soon after. I also found out that one sailor went down with the plane. What became of the other crew, I don't know. I wanted to at least talk to a Wren officer: 'Ma'am, could you please tell me what happened?' But I never did; you see, accidents like that, and worse, happened all the time, and people were dying all over the place, so you didn't question these things, you just got on with your job.

I didn't ever fly again. I went back to the storage section and continued to work on aircraft, and eventually I was upgraded to Petty Officer Wren, and was put in charge of the air radio stores. I was sent on a refresher course to HMS *Aerial*, which was in Warrington, and, while there, I was confirmed into the Church of England in Liverpool Cathedral by the Bishop of Warrington, which was something I'd been thinking a lot about, so that was quite a milestone. I was discharged in January 1946.

I wouldn't have missed the experience of the Wrens for the world, because it broadened my horizons, I met so many nice people from all over the country, I became more confident, gained a bit of knowledge, and, of course, I know how to wire a plug, if need be.

It had always been my ambition to see a Walrus again, and the opportunity came a few summers ago when I was having a holiday in Somerset with a friend. I said, 'If you don't mind, I would love to visit the Fleet Air Arm Museum in Yeovilton,' and she agreed. Well, if you could have seen my face when I came to this Walrus. I was thrilled to bits. Apparently there are only four left in the world, and this was one of them. I was a bit naughty and stepped over the rope to go and look through the window, and I could see where I would have been sitting: it looked very cramped, just a ledge where the wireless would have been, and me sat behind it, looking up into the cockpit.

The year before last I was idly reading through a magazine and came across this article about the Goldfish Club, and how to join it you had to be someone who had ditched in the sea and been rescued. As I was reading it, I was thinking, That's me, that's me. I was so excited, and I rang the Goldfish Club and told them a little bit about what had happened to me, and right away the Secretary said, 'Yes, of course you could be a member, and you would be a very rare commodity as a lady Goldfish.' So I sent everything off, and they eventually accepted me as a member.

Following that, I was thrilled to be one of six Goldfish invited by the Not Forgotten Association to a Garden Party at Buckingham Palace.

I had a wonderful send-off from home that day; I belong to a keep-fit class, full of lovely friends, and as a surprise they got together that morning to see me off to the Palace. My friend Joan had a Union Jack, which she waved, which was such fun, and as I drove off in a taxi – very extravagant, I know – I did a royal wave back to them. I got on the train with a very smart hat, and nicely dressed for a garden party. Of course no one dresses like that any more, so I was sitting on the train feeling very conspic- uous. I thought someone might say, 'Are you going to a wedding?' But no one took any notice of me. I was a bit disap- pointed. Anyway, I got to Liverpool Street, and took another taxi from there to Buckingham Palace. I thought, I shall indulge myself today.

I got into the beautiful gardens, and the six of us Goldfish sat in a little row, and then the band started playing, and the Duke of Gloucester came in with the Yeoman of the Guard, and I was presented to him, and he was very nice and kind, and asked me a few questions. After that we were led away to get tea from the marquee, where tables were set out everywhere with lovely dainty sandwiches and cakes, and all these young Armed Forces people were there to help you if you looked lost. So that was a really lovely day, but by the time I got home I was really, really tired.

I hope to be ninety-one in September. I am blessed because I have always been a sporty person right from childhood, and been a proper keep-fitter all these years, so I have kept the body going. But I haven't been too well the last year; little things keep cropping up, and in that time I have lost quite a bit of weight, and I look at myself in the mirror and think, well, you are really old now, Norah. But at the same time I am very active. I am a Friend of Covent Garden, among other things, and I was at the final dress rehearsal for a wonderful triple bill at the Royal Ballet the other day, and it was absolutely terrific.

On reflection, I think the fact that I was concussed when I ditched might have been a blessing, because, if I had remembered more, the horror of it would have hit me, and I might have real nightmares about it. As it is, I do dream a lot, and there is always water in my dreams, although whether it stems from that incident, I don't know. Also, I don't like walking across a pier, or anywhere looking down through gaps and seeing water.

RAY PARKIN

This is actually one of the greatest adventures of your life . . .

My father was a very enthusiastic aviator and I used to go all over the place with him as a kid, which was fantastic. His navigation was the old-fashioned variety: if you wanted to know which way the wind was blowing, you would see which way the cows were standing in the field – 'arse to the wind', he called it.

And then, when I was a young man, I decided I had to learn to fly. I took time off from my business and lived flying for three weeks. I got my licence pretty quickly, and then began to fly all the time from my home in Alderney, in the Channel Islands. I had all manner of aeroplanes over the next two or three years but I was just flying to Cherbourg, Jersey and Southampton. It was too local: I needed to go further afield. So I got in touch with a French company that had a little factory near Clermont-Ferrand, in the lee of the Massif Central, which made very sleek, quite big single-engine aircraft, and went down to see them. The owner said, 'You want to go distance? We have got an aeroplane called a Baladou. That would be a wonderful buy for you; it was built for travelling in Africa.' Well, I took one look at it and it appealed to me immediately. In fact, it would appeal to anyone, it was absolutely gorgeous: hand-made, five-seater, spacious inside, masses of room for baggage as well. I said, 'That one's for me.'

So I got my map out and started to plan. Right, I'm going to do *that* this year, I'm going to do *this* next year, and started to travel all around Europe. I went south, to the Mediterranean and southern Spain, because I love the sun, and then I thought, hang on, Africa is only across the water, so I went down to Marrakesh and Tangier, and all those places along that coast. The thing is, when you get somewhere in a small aeroplane, the next place is only about half an hour away, so you keep going.

After a while I ran the engine out; you have got so many hours on an engine, about three thousand hours, and then you must change the engine or have it reconditioned. I bought a brand new engine, which was damned expensive, but then I thought, well, while I'm about it I must upgrade my radios, so I put in ten thousand pounds' worth of new radios, state-of-the-art stuff. That was a lot of money then, round about 1983.

I went up to London for a couple of days and bought a load of stuff, including some wonderful food from Harrods, marvellous meats and pâtés, for a meal that evening. I came back to Southampton where I had left the plane and did the complete check of the aircraft. When I did my engine checks, I noticed the oil temperature was slightly warmer than normal, but it was a very hot day, freakishly so for October, and I just put it down to that.

I took off from Southampton with absolutely no problem at all. I was flying up at three thousand feet – they like to keep you below the commercial traffic going to Alderney and you don't need to go very high on that route anyway.

I was three-quarters of the way there, so I had seventeen miles or so to run to Alderney, when suddenly, very suddenly, the cabin filled with nasty, smelly blue smoke. I could see out, but it was stinging my eyes. I immediately called a Mayday to Jersey: 'Mayday, Mayday, Golf Bravo Alpha, Golf Mike, reporting serious condition of the engine. I have smoke in the cabin and oil pressure is dropping,' which they would know automatically points to the engine stopping very shortly.

Emergencies are treated in this lovely calm way, the idea being they don't want the pilot to panic, and the guy who was handling me was a very cool character. 'Are you able to maintain height?' he asked.

'No, I'm not.'

My initial reaction was one of absolute shock and fear. And the next thing that crossed my mind was that if this aeroplane was going to catch fire, I would be jumping out of it. I wasn't going to sit there and burn to death. And for some reason I thought of those guys during the war who had that situation, many of them because they had been fired at by the enemy.

The engine was now beginning to clank a little bit. I could hear this brand new engine really labouring, which hurt: if you like cars or engines, that noise is painful.

I managed to pick up a little bit more height, but travelling much slower. In the meantime the Jersey controller said, 'Just stand by, and we will come back to you.' Eventually, about three or four minutes later, he came back to me, which seemed a very long time. I thought he had deserted me. It is very comforting to have somebody to speak to.

'OK, Golf, Mike, we have located you,' he said, 'and we have an aircraft that is going to be joining you shortly.' And, sure enough, this aircraft came along, about five or six hundred feet above me. It was an Aztec, a very nice twin-engined aircraft, on its way to Cherbourg, and they had diverted him to me. He was there to see what happened to me, so if there was an explosion, or anything like that, he could report it. Also, if you landed in the sea, the aircraft would very likely break up on impact and then sink, so it was very useful having an aircraft to watch and circle, and report.

I travelled on for a little longer and managed to maintain a certain amount of height, but then there was this horrible sound of the engine running out of oil, and I decided to get as close to the water as possible, because if there was going to be a fire I wanted to be able to get into the sea pronto. Going very strongly through my mind was the thought that I was probably going to die. But then something happened, which I still can't account for, but is absolutely true.

I had just lost my older brother, Stan; such a lovely guy, he died when he was fifty-two, much too young. I'd always had a great closeness to him. Suddenly, I could hear his voice perfectly clearly, and he was talking to me. 'Don't worry, Ray,' he was saying, 'just do the right things, and you'll be OK.'

He convinced me I was going to survive, and I suddenly got

a terrific feeling that I was going to get out of this. In fact, I felt a new spirit: *Ray, you can handle this, this is actually one of the greatest adventures of your life! Now, come on, enjoy it.*

I made sure the lifebelts and life jackets were near at hand, and pulled the dinghy forward and made sure the release rope was close. The thing they tell you about ditching procedure is to make sure nothing in the aircraft is loose. Well, I looked around and almost everything was stashed away, but I had a can of Coke, and a little wheel chock made of metal, which I would put under the front wheel in case I had to park on a slope, and I couldn't reach them, so I thought, OK, they will have to stay, but I had now more or less made myself ready for impact.

And then the engine conked out and the propeller stopped turning.

The thing about losing your engine is the extraordinary silence; you get a real feeling of wind rushing past, and that was quite exciting – to tell the truth, I now found everything exhilarating.

As we got closer to the sea, I decided to pull the canopy back – like a fighter aircraft – so then I would be able to get out quicker when we landed on the sea. But then my mind went back to the aviation classroom: *Do not under any circumstances pull the canopy back. If you pull the canopy back while flying, it will probably lock, and you will be stuck in the aircraft.* So I quickly chucked that idea out of the window. Then I thought again: well, shall I jump out before? But I realised that was idiotic, I'd kill myself. Stick with the aeroplane, Ray.

I was now at about one hundred feet. I could see the waves quite clearly. I got the speed down as low as I possibly could. It was a very calm day, visibility was about fifteen hundred feet, not a lot, and very hazy. Now I was flying at twenty-five or thirty feet over the water, doing about eighty knots. There's a tail skid on the back of the aircraft, and I thought, I'll put the tail skid into the water first. The water looked so calm and welcoming … When that tail skid went into the water it was like a sledgehammer hitting an anvil, the noise was incredible. BANG! There was a terrific impact, and the whole aeroplane shuddered.

Also, as we hit the water the can of Coke took off and was now bouncing all round the cabin, the metal chock was flying everywhere, pennies were tumbling all over the place, the spare life jackets were zooming past me, everything that could move was going round the cockpit like dice in a box, and if one of those things had hit me that would have been it. So that was another lesson learned.

I only had a seatbelt: I didn't have an upper torso restraint, which you have in every plane nowadays. Well, on impact with the water my whole body shot forward and I hit my head on the control panel, and I was knocked unconscious for a short time, probably no more than thirty seconds or so. When I eventually came to, I was floating nose down. The Aztec had seen me go in and he made off. I was in the middle of Hurd's Deep, one of the deepest troughs in the world. I remember hearing about a submarine, called the *Affray*, going down there in the early 1950s with total loss of life – and they were never able to retrieve it because it was just too deep. Nobody could get down that far.

Well, first of all I thanked God for being alive. 'Thank you very much, Lord, for saving me.' Then I sat there for a minute, and thought, well, what happens next? I tried the canopy. That went back all right. I put my life jacket on. I had my dinghy right next to me. Suddenly, I thought, oh my God, the dinghy ... I had just bought it at a party from a friend who'd bought a new one. He had asked £150 for it, and I'd said, 'Let's do double or quits, if I lose I'll give you £300 for it, if I win, it's mine, for nothing.' We tossed the coin – I got it for nothing! I hadn't checked it, though, and I suddenly wondered, what am I going to find when I pull that cord, a bag of sawdust? That did worry me. So I put the dinghy outside and pulled the cord. Up it came, absolutely perfect; it even had a little zipped entrance on it, and I can tell you it looked like the entrance to the Savoy Hotel to me, it was just so beautiful floating there. I looked inside, and it had water-making equipment, emergency biscuits, a sack of food, and even a little cape to put on to keep warm.

What should I do now? My baggage was in the rear hold, with all that wonderful food from Harrods, and I thought, I'll just nip round in the dinghy and get those out. Why lose it? They were expensive. So I got all that. Then, greed, avarice, set in ... I thought, I have just put ten thousand pounds' worth of radio into this aircraft, I wonder if I can get that out? So I got back into the aircraft, and the water was now up to my knees, but I knew how to get aircraft radios out: you do it with an Allen key, and simply take them out of the slots. Damn, I hadn't got an Allen key. But I had a Scout knife, which was a dangerous looking thing, and I thought, if I can get the sharp end of that knife into the hole for the Allen key, the radio will come out. So I put the knife in and tried to prise out the radio, and the knife slipped and I stabbed myself in my hand; the blade went straight through my hand and out the other side.

I quickly pulled it out, blood was going everywhere, and I put my hand in the salt water, which was now waist-high. I thought, what am I doing? I have just escaped death after crashing into the sea, and now I am trying to stab myself to death, this is crazy, you are insured, for God's sake; and I was so annoyed with myself I just put my head in my hands.

But then I heard a helicopter, and out of the mist came this lovely old Wessex. The winchman came down and tried to get to my dinghy – but he missed and ended up in the sea, he actually went under the water. Anyway, eventually he emerged from the water and said, 'Hang on to me', and pulled me up, and I just left everything behind in the dinghy. As we were going up, the downstream from the rotors started to whizz us around; we were soon going round and round like Whirling Dervishes, which might have been comical except I was getting dizzy. And then we hit the undercarriage and I got a real clunk on the leg, and I'm not sure that should have happened. This guy just didn't seem to know what he was doing.

Eventually, though, we were pulled into the Wessex and we headed back to Portland. We were just picking up speed nicely, when, without warning, a plastic window right next to me shot out and zoomed straight past my head; it could have cut my throat as it went by. The winchman said, 'Sorry about the window, mate, but we were servicing the aircraft when we got the Mayday, so we didn't complete the servicing. In fact, I am not really a winchman.' And I thought, now I understand why you disappeared into the water . . .

They dropped me in a field where two policemen were waiting for me in a police car, and they took me to Weymouth

Hospital. This very nice sister said, 'Lie down for a minute, the doctor is coming to see you.'

'But there's nothing wrong with me, I haven't got any injury except for my hand.'

'Just hold on,' she said, and she brought me a mirror. I looked terrible. My face was absolutely covered in blood, the whole of my forehead and behind my ears was congealed blood; it was everywhere. I thought, where the hell did that come from? And then I realised: I had been spreading blood from my hand when I cupped my head in my hands. Anyway, they had a quick look at my hand, gave me antibiotics and said they could let me go.

By that time it was early evening. 'Do you want us to get you a taxi?' they asked, and I said, 'No, I would rather walk, it is such a lovely evening.'

So there I was in Weymouth, just thinking what a wonderful place the world was, and I thought, I shall make my way to a church and say an official thank you to whoever is up there. I couldn't find a church anywhere, but I heard voices coming from a pub so I went in. There were about six guys there, obviously local, and as I walked in they all turned to see who was coming in. I didn't say anything at first, I felt becalmed almost. I ordered a beer. I polished my drink off. That pint of beer was delicious, absolutely wonderful! 'Gentlemen,' I said, 'would you like to join me for a drink?' And one of them said, 'Thanks mate', and the others did as well. They were splendid chaps, salt of the earth. And then after we had finished our drinks, I said, 'Goodnight gentlemen, it's a great world!' Afterwards, I thought they probably reckoned I was some sort of nutter who had just escaped from a home.

I wasn't scared or discouraged from flying; in fact, I started flying the next week. But about a year after the ditching I did have a bit of heart trouble, misspent youth probably, and had some stents put in. I had to report that to the CAA medical authorities and they said, 'We're afraid we can't reissue you with another licence.' So I just got on with my life. I am part-owner of an aircraft now, so I can fly dual, although, of course, it's not quite the same. I still miss flying terrifically.

DOUG REICH

'Welcome Home, Doug . . .'

A prisoner-of-war picture

It was a Sunday morning and we were listening to the radio at home, and on came the bulletin with Neville Chamberlain saying we hadn't received a reply from our note to Adolf Hitler, so we were now at war.

My father was quite upset. 'Oh, not again,' he said. He had been a prisoner of war in the First World War; he'd been a machine-gunner in France, and all I know is that the Germans overran his position and he was taken prisoner, and when he came back he was half starved.

I had just turned seventeen at that time; I was apprenticed in the newspaper industry as a photoengraver on the *Daily Herald*, and so I got all the latest information about the war through that, and got quite interested in what was going on. I had a pal who was exactly the same age as me, and on the weekends we used to go for long walks through the woods at Worsley, near Manchester, discussing the war, and eventually we decided to volunteer rather than wait for a call-up, where you wouldn't have any choice at all. So off we went to Manchester and volunteered.

They asked me if I would like to volunteer for aircrew duties, and I said yes, although I had never even seen an aeroplane. Well, you might have done if you lived in London or Croydon, but in the north of England you just didn't. They then sent me home to await further instructions, and, a few weeks later, I was noti-fied to go to RAF Cardington in the Midlands, where I spent three days taking medical, intelligence and psychological tests, and when that finished I went before a Board of Examiners. A group of officers were sat behind a great big desk and started throwing questions at me. What sort of sport did I like? What books did I read? And while I was giving my answers, suddenly this group captain pulled out a revolver, and pointed it at me – and I shot under the desk; I was pretty lively in those days. He said, 'You can come out now', and when I came out, I could hear everybody laughing. This group captain said, 'Well, I have pulled that stunt a few times, but I've never seen anybody move as fast as that in all my life.' He went on to explain I had passed all the tests, and they were recommending me for training as a pilot. So, back home again, and another wait for further orders.

Eventually, I got a call to go to the aircrew reception centre at St John's Wood cricket ground in London. There were hundreds of us there, and eventually we got sorted into batches of 120, and we were marched off by a corporal to billets in St John's Wood, very posh flats, which had been commandeered by the RAF.

In March '42, about seven hundred of us went by train up to Gourock on the Clyde in Scotland, and we boarded this American Liberty ship that had been converted to be a troop carrier, and they split us, half in the forward hold and half in the stern hold. There were endless rows of metal latticed bunk beds, four tiers high, hanging on metal stanchions, and plenty of spare chains dangling down, and, at night, with the ship rolling and pitching, all the chains rattling, and blokes moaning because they were sick, it was like the Black Hole of Calcutta. There were thirteen merchant ships in the convoy, and it took us thirteen days to cross the Atlantic. Apparently the convoy which had left about four days in front of us had been badly mauled by a U-boat pack and lost a lot of ships. I was sleeping right on the waterline of the ship, with the waves bashing against it, so I wouldn't have stood a chance if we'd been torpedoed.

Eventually we sailed up past the Statue of Liberty into New York, and then into Brooklyn Navy Yard, where the Americans had everything very well organised, and the next morning we boarded a train up to Montreal. It was about four o'clock in the morning when we arrived, and on the station platform they had a great big temperature gauge, which said nineteen below. They warned us not to touch any metal, and to keep our gloves on, but it was so dry it didn't really feel cold.

Our first weekend they gave us a pass into Montreal. I had the equivalent of about ninety pounds English money, which I'd changed into Canadian dollars, and that was a great deal of money to have saved, because the RAF pay was coppers, really.

The main street in Montreal is Sainte-Catherine Street, and we wandered around looking at the sights. We passed a shop that sold fresh orange juice: oranges were being fed through an automatic squeezer into a big glass tank, and out was coming these glasses of pure orange juice. Well, we hadn't seen oranges for ages, and the orange juice tasted like nectar. We then went into the first restaurant we saw and ordered lamb chops. A great big plate arrived with four whacking big chops on it, and then another plate loaded with vegetables. After the rationing in England we couldn't get at it quick enough.

Then I was sent to flying school at a place called Windsor Mills, about ninety miles from Montreal, and the food was excellent there too. Well, at that age food means everything ... They had proper civilian cooks, and you could have anything you wanted; for instance, for breakfast we had pancakes with maple syrup, and they had the lightweight stuff or the dark syrup, which was as thick as molasses, then as many eggs as you wanted, plus a load of bacon.

I was introduced to my instructor; he was a hell of a nice fellow on the ground, but when he got into the cockpit with a pupil, I don't know whether it was nerves or what but he never stopped yattering and complaining. My plane was a Fleet Finch, a biplane like a Tiger Moth, but with a five-cylinder radial engine, two seats fore and aft, with the pupil in the front seat and the instructor in the back. This fellow took me up and threw the thing all over the sky, did all sorts of aerobatics. We landed, and he said, 'How do you feel, son?', and I had to admit I was feeling a bit sick. The next morning we did a couple of landings, and he said, 'Do you think you can get this fucking plane up in the air [he swore like a trooper] and back in one piece?' I said, 'I'm sure I can.' So he got out of the back cockpit and I took off solo.

He must have notified the ground crews he was going to send me off, because as I taxied round to take off out came two fire engines and an ambulance, waiting for me to come in to land . . . He was obviously full of confidence as to my abilities.

Anyway, I took off, went round the circuit and made a perfect landing. Out he comes and congratulates me, and, as we walked past the other instructors he stuck his chest out, strutting he was, and he said to them, 'That's the way to teach these lads to fly.'

We then began flying Harvards. The Harvard was much more advanced than a Fleet Finch, but all you needed was to get used to the controls and the instruments, and then they would send you up solo, which I did. Off I went, but when I came in to land, something was wrong; red flares were going up all over the place, and they wouldn't let us land, although by that time there were about twenty Harvards circling around. Anyway, I circled with the rest of them and then I noticed there was a Harvard burning on the runway. After about half an hour or so they cleared it to one side, and after I landed I went past this burning wreck. When I got in, I found out it was my instructor.

So then I got another instructor, Flying Officer Thompson,

nice fellow, meticulous bloke, and very keen; the first aircraft off in the morning was always him. One morning he got in the back seat, and said, 'Right, we'll go and do some aerobatics,' and off we went to a special area to do it. We got to about thirteen or fourteen thousand feet, and started doing steep turns and loops, and all that sort of thing. After about an hour, he said, 'That's enough, take it down, and we'll go and do some forced landings.'

If you come down steadily it takes a long time; the quickest way is to put the aircraft into a spin. So I put it in a spin: throttle back, lift the nose up until it starts to stall, and then, whichever rudder you put on, that's the way you spin. I pulled out at about seven thousand feet, and went to open the throttle full, and it wouldn't move: solid it was. From the back seat came, 'Open the throttle.'

'I'm trying to, it won't move.'

'Right, I'll have control,' he said. But he was coupled up with my throttle, so if mine wouldn't move nor would his. Next thing, there's a whacking big explosion, and a sheet of flames came out of the engine. 'Right, bail out, bail out!' I undid my safety harness, unplugged my intercom lead, took my helmet off, climbed out of the aircraft and stood on the wing, hanging on to the cockpit, looking down at these little patchwork fields thousands of feet beneath us. And then, just at that moment, the shoulder straps of my harness fell off – they were too loose. I knew before we'd taken off that they needed adjusting, but the blinking parachute section was about a mile across the airfield, and to lug the parachute all that way, well, I never got round to it. The flames had gone out by now, the engine was just smoking, so I jumped back in the cockpit. But now the engines had stopped completely and

116

the instructor said, 'Go through the forced landing procedure.' Harvards don't glide very well because they are heavy, but the procedure for a forced landing is to come down in a figure of eight, pick out some nice big fields and when you get to the edge of the field you should be in a position to either land, coming in from the right, or turn on your figure of eight and come in from the left, so you've got two chances to get in. In the meantime, I was looking for my instructor in my mirror, and I couldn't see him. I thought, What the hell is he doing? This is an emergency and he's the instructor, but I'm doing all the flying. Then, just as I turned in on this field, up he bobs and says, 'I have control,' and he belly-landed in this field, where we bumped along a bit, and then we jumped out. No damage done, except to the plane.

In December 1942 I finally received a commission as a pilot officer and came back to England, and then I had to go before a Board at Harrogate. The first thing they said was, 'I'm afraid there's no call for fighter pilots right now, as Fighter Command is full, but we can offer you Army Co-operation Command; how would you like to join that? They fly in Mustangs, so you'll need your navigation skills for that.' OK, I said, that's fine.

The purpose was to work closely with the Army, who would send us out for reconnaissance. We carried an oblique camera in the cockpit just behind the pilot's seat, and we took photographs from low down; all our flying was done very low down. There was a control box on the floor of the cockpit, and you could just switch it on and set the shutter, and it would take about two hundred pictures, one after the other. And the Mustang was great; compared to the Harvards, it was like a Ferrari after a Ford 8, really lovely to fly.

The first operation I did was across to the Frisian Islands. The Germans were sneaking ships around the islands with supplies, plus they had a torpedo squadron on the coast all bombed up and ready. So we went out doing reconnaissance, looking for them, and if we saw anything we could radio back and give their positions so our boys could send planes out and attack the convoy.

The invasion was on 6 June, and one of our jobs was to 'spot' for the guns firing at the coastal batteries. We were cruising around above these guns, watching for the explosion of the shells and sending corrections to the cruisers: 'Up two hundred yards, left one hundred yards,' helping the gunners to hit a target somewhere. And then, later on, I went out on a reconnaissance looking for a German Panzer division, which was in the area somewhere, although we couldn't find it.

The invasion area was the Cherbourg Peninsula. This Army captain asked if we could bring some bread for these fellows who'd been building a runway there, and living on hard tack biscuits for a fortnight, to which I reluctantly agreed. We were due to take off at ten o'clock in the morning, and I was sat in the cockpit, and had started the engine, with my no. 2 in the plane behind me, when up comes this little Austin van from the mess hall, and a sergeant comes out with loads of bread in a basket. Well, the cockpit's only small – in fact your head is touching the canopy when you are sat in it – but he piled endless loaves in and I had to take off with all this bread around me.

It was the first time I had been over the invasion beaches, so I had a good look around, and then I thought, I had better land and deliver this bread. So there was this sandy strip, and I put my wheels down, banged about thirty degrees of flap, throttled back and landed. I taxied to the end of the runway, with clouds of dust and sand going up everywhere, got to the end, and nobody was there at all. So I turned around and taxied back, under clouds of dust again, to the other end. Nobody there either. So I'm getting quite annoyed by now, and then a chap jumps up out of a foxhole and comes running across. 'The Germans are sniping at us from the trees over there,' he said, 'that's why we're all in foxholes.' I thought, blimey, I'd better get out of this place pretty quick, so I gave him the bread and we took off.

We were flying at fifteen hundred feet, just to see if we could spot any tanks hidden in the trees. It was a beautiful day, clear blue sky, blazing hot sun, and we covered a fair bit of ground. And then my no. 2 called me up and said, 'I've seen something at eleven o'clock high.' I looked up, but in the blazing sun I couldn't see a thing. So I started a turn towards where he had seen something, and, as we turned, about nine Focke-Wulf 190s came hurtling out of the sun. If my no. 2 hadn't warned me, they would have knocked me off as easy as killing flies. I went over on my back, straight down, full throttle to the deck, then pulled out, skimming the trees and cutting the grass on the fields. The Germans were spread out at the back, but the Mustang in a dive picks up speed very quickly, and I was now doing near five hundred miles an hour, so they couldn't catch me. I then started leading them into the beachhead, because I knew there were two squadrons of Spitfires circling up there, but after such a violent manoeuvre my radio mast had snapped off, so the radio was useless and I couldn't contact them. So I just gave up and flew back to Gatwick.

I then got briefed to attack ferry boats on the River Seine.

The French Underground had been on to tell us that, because there were dozens of Allied fighters and fighter bombers circling around, the Germans couldn't move anything on the road, so to get the troops to the beachhead at night they were ferrying troops north across the Seine.

We took off early in the morning and flew out to a place called Caudebec, on the banks of the Seine. The river there was about half a mile wide, and I came low over some trees doing three hundred-odd miles an hour, dropped on the water, and there was one of these ferry boats. At this stage I was lower than his deck, so I couldn't miss, and I gave him a good squirt with four 20mm cannons, which must have done a fair bit of damage, and then pulled up to let my no. 2, who was behind me, have a go. I then looked back and saw another ferry boat on the bank, which had just come over, and I put my nose down and went at him, gave him a squirt and then decided to fly further along the Seine.

I pulled over in a very tight turn low down on the river, and that's the last thing I remember . . .

I don't know what happened. I know I wasn't hit by aircraft fire, because I would have felt that. So either I pulled up and turned too tight and stalled, in which case I would have flopped into the river, or I was so low down that I put a wing tip in the water and cartwheeled in. But I can't remember anything. I lost all memory for about the next ten hours, until I woke up in this little cottage hospital at Caudebec.

Immediately I thought, there's something funny going on here, but I couldn't make out what it was, and then I suddenly realised I couldn't see. What had happened, I later found out, was that when the aircraft hit the water, it shot me out, and all the blood rushed from my body up to my head, and burst all the blood vessels in my eyes. The blood from these tiny vessels had now congealed and my eyelids wouldn't open. Eventually, I got one eye open and was able to take stock of the situation. I was lying next to a window, and there was a drive, and at the end of the drive were some wrought-iron gates and a German guard on duty with his steel helmet and rifle.

There was an Austrian doctor in charge of my ward, a nice fellow, who hated the Nazis. He had been a third-year medical student, and when the Nazis had taken over in Austria he'd got pushed into the Medical Corps, which is how he landed up in this hospital. But he hated the Nazis: all he was interested in was when the war would finish. He told me what had happened to me, that I had gone in the water about half past nine in the morning, and that some time in the afternoon a French boat had fished me out of the water, unconscious; they thought maybe I was dead. So they handed me over to the Germans, and the Germans found out I was still alive and brought me to this hospital.

Anyway, later on in the day someone said, 'You are going to Rouen now,' and carted me down on a stretcher to the forecourt where an ambulance was waiting. Unfortunately, it only had four slots for stretchers, and they were occupied by Germans – they might well have been fellows off this ferry boat I had hit – so I was dumped on the floor. But this Austrian medic, who was senior ranking, played merry hell, shouting away, and eventually one of these Germans was pulled off the ambulance rack and put on the floor, and I was given a rack. Not bad going.

I don't remember anything about the journey, but next day I

woke up in the hospital at Rouen. They had put me in a ward all on my own, and I was bursting to empty my bladder. I shouted, but nobody came. I had banged my leg in the crash, and from the knee down it was swollen and battered, and all the colours of the rainbow, and aching like mad; plus my ankle was broken and I couldn't walk on it. But I managed to get out of bed and crawl down this ward, and get through the door into the corridor, where I shouted out for attention. Eventually a nurse came and carted me back into bed, and brought me a bottle, which I promptly filled, much to my happiness.

The next night they moved me to Paris on a rickety old bus. They had put a splint on my leg, but they were short of bandages so they used paper. I don't know how far it is from Rouen to Paris, but this old bus bounced around so much that by the time I got to Paris the paper bandages had burst and the splint had fallen off.

They put me in a ward in this very modern hospital, which the Luftwaffe had taken over, and in came this big German surgeon with his entourage to examine me. He never looked at my leg, which was the thing causing me all the trouble, but began looking at the whites of my eyes, which were blood-red. There was also a bit of a lump on my head, which I'd banged. He had a little mallet and he kept tapping my head while talking to his crew.

Eventually he decided what was wrong, and they put me on a trolley and wheeled me into the operating theatre and laid me out on the table. They had glass cabinets all the way round the wall, and you never saw such a load of instruments; frightening they were, chisels, hammers and saws, and I thought, What the hell are they going to do? Anyway, the surgeon then came in with his team, ready to operate. He stuck my X-ray up on a screen, backed away, had another look, then he called a couple of fellows over, and they had a confab, while I'm laid on this table. In the end, he banged me on the head, and said, 'Get the Englishmen out of here.' Apparently there was nothing wrong with me.

They took me to the seventh floor where they had a prison ward with bars on the windows. There were two beds in each cubicle, and the fellow in the other bed of my cubicle was a bomber off a Lancaster who had bailed out and landed on a roof and broken his back, so he couldn't move. He was a Yorkshire lad, and I'm a Lancashire lad, but we got on all right, under the circumstances. I slept like a log anyway most of the time, which apparently you do with concussion. I just couldn't stay awake.

The next morning, this German orderly came up and said, 'You'll have to get up now, you're going to Germany.' I got up, but I couldn't put my foot on the floor, I was in terrible pain. 'It's no good,' I said, 'I can't walk.' So off he goes and comes back with a bowl of water, and mixes this plaster and bandage and puts it round my ankle. I still couldn't walk very well, so I asked him for a crutch, and all he did was go out in the grounds of the hospital and cut a branch off a tree for a walking stick, which wasn't very good because it cut my hands.

They took us then by truck to the mainline station in Paris. There were only three of us; there was an American fighter pilot who had bailed out of a Thunderbolt just as it exploded, and the flames had caught his face and hands, and the other one was a gunner from a Flying Fortress, and he was limping, so I think he had hurt his leg.

And then a couple of German guards came into the compartment, and they were to escort us to Germany. One was a real nasty piece of work, he wouldn't do anything for us. It was a red-hot day, and we were stuck in this compartment, and when we asked for a drink of water, no, he wouldn't get one. He had a big bottle of champagne with him, and he just sat in the corner and got drunk on this stuff, and in the end, when we pulled into the station, he was fast asleep and snoring his head off. The other guard was OK, and got some water for us in a billycan.

They unloaded us at a place called Oberursel, which was an interrogation centre. I ended up in solitary confinement in this blinking prison cell, with a tatty old straw mattress and one blanket. I know I was interrogated there, but I don't actually remember anything about it.

From there I went to a transit camp, and then on to a train; we were three days on this train, in fact, and eventually finished up on the Baltic coast at Stalag Luft I, which was an Air Force POW camp between Rostock and Stettin. I couldn't walk properly, so there was nothing I could do about escaping. I just accepted what was going on. But I was lucky to be sent to Stalag Luft I. The majority of prisoners had been sent to Stalag Luft III in Poland, and before the Russians came through they were marched hundreds and hundreds of miles, no matter what condition they were in, and a lot of them died on those marches.

Stalag Luft I was just a bunch of wooden huts surrounded by barbed wire and sentry towers; in my room there were four Poles, two Norwegians, a South African, a couple of Australians and the rest were RAF. I was in that camp for eleven months.

The Germans shut the light off about nine o'clock, so from

nine o'clock you were supposed to be in darkness, but we made little candles out of American margarine from the American food parcels; Olay Oil it was called, which looked and tasted like axle grease, terrible stuff, honestly it was. But we melted the margarine into tin lids, cut a bit of boot lace for a wick and had about half a dozen of those burning round the table while we played cards. We played cribbage for a cigarette a point – we used cigarettes as the currency in the camp. All the food had a cigarette number rate for buying and selling, so if you had plenty of cigarettes and fancied a bit of chocolate you could trade so many cigarettes for a bar of chocolate made by the American Air Force, which was full of calories. D Bars, they were called.

I was a clever bugger, and won hands down at cards, and soon had piles of cigarettes, and exchanged them all for jam, cheese and chocolate from the Red Cross parcels, and ate the lot. Of course everyone's luck changes after a while, and I started losing, and then I owed cigarettes. I hadn't got them because I had traded them all for food, so when the Red Cross parcels came I had to sell mine to pay my debts, so I went hungry, which taught me a lesson about gambling.

We would have starved without these parcels, because the Germans were giving us very little food; potatoes were the main thing, and a lot of the time they weren't too clever, but we had to eat them anyway. I feel very grateful to the Red Cross.

Well, our main concern, of course, was getting back home, and we always wanted to know how the war was going. We got the BBC one o'clock news. Some of these lads were very clever, and in no time at all they had built a radio. The Germans kept having a go at finding it; they had a special team of 'ferrets', as we called them, and sometimes when we came back to our hut after exercise the ferrets had been searching and turned everything upside down, trying to find this radio.

Every time the post came, everybody crowded round waiting for a letter. We had one lad whose wife was very pregnant when he was shot down, and he didn't know whether he was a father or not, and eventually, several months later, he did get a letter to say he had a son, and he was absolutely over the moon. But there were also the Dear John letters; you've never seen anything like it. I remember a letter received from a wife saying, 'Dear John, everything is all right, but I have had a baby by an American captain, not to worry though, he's a nice fellow ...'

One day, towards the end of the war, the German commandant came to see the senior officers in charge of our section of the camp. Our Senior Allied Officers were a very famous American fighter pilot, called Colonel Hubert 'Hub' Zemke, and a group captain from the RAF. This German commandant said, 'The Russians are on the way, so I've had instructions to march you out. We will leave tomorrow.' I suppose this fellow was desperate for his own safety, knowing what the Russians would do to him. Anyway, our chaps said, 'We're not moving.' And the commandant said, 'Well, that's up to you ...' And during the night all the German guards left, so we took over the camp ourselves. We now had our own blokes on the gate, which is just as well because one night a load of drunken Russians came through, firing guns and all sorts; they were a right rabble, but we saw them off. And then a second group of Russians came in, and some colonel or other had a look round the camp, and really wanted to help us, and he eventually decreed we hadn't got any fresh meat. So the following day, up the road to the main camp gate comes a drunken Russian with a Tommy gun, driving about thirty cows he had taken from some farm somewhere. A lot of the Americans were farm boys, and they were out milking them in no time at all.

A couple of days later, about thirty Flying Fortresses, American daylight bombers, came circling in and landed on this field. They were stripped of everything; all they carried was a pilot, a navigator and a wireless operator, so they could pack us into these old bombers. The Americans very graciously said that the RAF personnel could go first, so we marched up to this field and climbed in the planes. About three got off, and the fourth one ran off the perimeter track, some idiot pilot got his wheel stuck into the soft ground and down it went, and we couldn't shift it. About three hundred of us got ropes and were trying to pull this damn thing out, and then eventually we commandeered a couple of tractors from a local farmer and they got it out. But this had been going on all day long, and it was now late afternoon, and I got quite worried because I thought, these American pilots only fly in daylight, I bet this guy has never flown at night, and it's going to be dark by the time we get back to England, and we're going to crash on the runway and all get killed. But I really maligned the poor fellow, because he made a lovely landing.

Incidentally, on our way up to that airfield we found a miniature Belsen alongside it, with about three or four thousand prisoners who were there to service the airfield. They were all skeletons, and they had typhoid, and were dying every day, so the doctor wouldn't let anyone go in there. But we did talk to one young fellow of about eighteen. Somebody offered him a cigarette, and he could hardly lift his arm up to take a drag he was that weak, which was pretty shocking.

We landed around two o'clock in the morning at Ford on the south coast, and they told us to get some sleep. They interviewed us the following morning. They wanted our number and all that sort of thing, and I couldn't remember mine, which was still part of the concussion, I think. It actually took me a long time to recover from the concussion; my memory was really screwed up. Then they gave us a clean battledress and shirts, and a travel warrant. I phoned home and said I'd be arriving about four o'clock at Manchester Piccadilly, and my father came and picked me up.

There was a banner outside our house, saying 'Welcome Home Doug' strung across the front window, and my father had a special bottle of whisky he'd saved for when I came home, so we had a nice evening supping this whisky. But my mother was in bed. She'd had a stroke and was recovering from it, but I think the excitement of me coming home was a bit too much for her, and about fourteen days afterwards she had another stroke, and never recovered consciousness, which is a pity because I never really got close to her again. I was away from 1941 until 1946, so I hadn't seen much of my family, and then I lost my mother just as I got back, which was sad really.

Nearly every night I think about my ditching, because I am still trying to get back what happened to me. I go through it in my dreams too . . . sometimes I am flying across to France, and getting close to the Seine where I ditched, and hoping the dream will carry on . . . but it always stops as I am turning on the river, and then it's completely blank until I wake up in the little cottage hospital.

Of course, all this was a long time ago. I went to war as a boy; I mean, as a young fellow of seventeen you haven't seen anything of life at all, but when this sort of thing goes on, and you see terrible things happen, you quickly grow up, and I definitely came back to England a man.

Well, you can't do anything about getting old, and I'm an old man now, but at my age, which is ninety, you can more or less do what you like, and if you are being a bit silly, people will say, 'Silly old bugger, take no notice of him.' Actually, I would like to reach a hundred, providing I am still fit. I wouldn't want to be staggering around, or mental, or anything like that. But I am fairly fit now, I do the garden, and cut three lawns regularly, and I've not had any serious illness, touch wood, so I am rather pleased with myself.

ARCHIE NAUGHTON

'Shaken not stirred . . . '

I had always liked the idea of flying, and I came into the Navy as a helicopter pilot and really enjoyed my work. I ended up flying the Wessex 5, which was big and noisy compared to the complex machines now, and getting on a bit even in those days, but a venerable workhorse. On the plus side, it was stable and relatively easy to fly, it could be used for search and rescue, or dropping underslung loads, ammunition or Land Rovers, and it was also big enough to take a stick of marines, who we would drop off at landing sites.

Our home at one time was HMS *Bulwark*, a purpose-built fixed-wing aircraft carrier which had been converted to a commando carrier sometime in the sixties. There were eight circles marked on the deck, and the aircraft would come up from the hangar and be positioned to the spots that were allocated to them for that day.

On 16 January 1976 we were somewhere near the Azores. It was a bright, sunny and pleasant morning; the whole flight deck was lined up – all the spots were filled that day – so aircraft were burning and turning all over the place. The squadron was up for whatever we were doing.

We were tasked to do missile training: to go off and choose a target, pretend to fire a missile, but just guide it with the joystick and then come back again. My crew had been together for a while; helicopters are normally flown from the right-hand seat, so Mike Crabtree, the pilot, was sitting on the right, I was next to him, with the missile sight in front of me, and at the back of the aircraft, facing out to the side, was Soapy Watson, Leading Aircrewman Watson.

By great good fortune we were on spot 1, which was at the very front of the aircraft carrier, so there was nothing between the bow and us. Spot 1 was slightly different from the others because you could come up into the hover and then transition away, left or right. What we used to do was come up in the hover – and disappear off the end of the flight deck – which for a few seconds scared the ship's lieutenant-commander in Flyco, the command and control authority housed in the island over-looking the flight deck, because for that short period of time he wouldn't quite know what had happened to you. We were young and silly.

So we came up for take-off, and immediately transitioned for-ward over the ship. But this time, even for me, I thought we were staying there a touch too long and I looked across to Mike to say, 'OK Mike, that's enough,' and I shall never forget the look of complete horror on his face, because he had the stick fully back in his stomach, so the aircraft should have been rotating upwards, but very clearly it wasn't, and when I looked back, the sea, instead of being horizontal, was effectively at right angles. In other words, we were plunging head first directly into the sea at seventy knots, which is about eighty to eighty-five miles per hour, and water is quite hard when you hit it at that speed.

It's very hard to describe the violence of the impact: people who heard and saw it said they were sure we were going to be killed and were amazed we had survived.

The next thing was we were under the water. Now, we had trained for this in the underwater escape trainer, back at Yeovilton RNAS, because the Navy has historically had some difficulties with people surviving accidents, and then drowning. The sequence is: you put one hand on your seatbelt quick-release box, you take another hand and put it somewhere that will orientate you, because you won't know whether the aircraft is upside down or whatever direction, you wait until everything stabilises and then pull yourself out. Finally, you allow your natural buoyancy to get you to the surface, and you don't attempt to swim because you could be swimming the wrong way.

But with all this going through our heads, all of a sudden, rather comically, the aircraft came up to the surface, because it had flotation packs on its wheels that were activated by salt water, at which point Mike and I just looked at each other and smiled. It was a sort of 'Well, that was all right then, shaken not stirred' moment, a bit of an adventure. Then Mike said to me, 'Where's Watson?' and right at that moment, from the back of the aircraft, where he shouldn't really have been – he must have been thrown back by the impact – a little head popped out of a window and all he said was, 'Fucking hell!'

However, a rather ominous event was developing: I heard this swish, and I looked up and our ship was just above us, and, in addition to that, it was turning away, which is fine, except that six hundred feet later the stern would be starting to come out towards us and would mow us down. I remember thinking, dear God, I've just survived this, and now I'm going to be run down by my own ship! But, amazingly, it didn't hit us.

Then the search and rescue aircraft, another Wessex, which was always standing by while at sea, got airborne. It came round and we jumped into the water, put the strap on and were winched up and back on to the ship. The whole thing, from the launching of the SAR to getting airborne, took about ten minutes.

Our helicopter was pretty comprehensively damaged. The rear section was gone completely, the tail rotor section had just disappeared and the nose of the aircraft had gone down too, windows were wrecked, the rotor blades were literally smashed down from twenty feet to three or four feet, and the exhausts from the turbo engines were squashed into a crescent from the violence of the impact.

As we came off the aircraft on to the ship, they immediately impounded our safety equipment, life jackets, crash helmets, even our flying overalls as part of the inquiry, along with technical things, like the log of the aircraft. We were then taken down to sickbay, assessed by a doctor and then immediately taken to a Board of Inquiry, literally within minutes. It was just a change of clothes, and then, 'Let's go down and have this Board.'

The only thing I can remember about the inquiry now was the Commander of the Air Engineering Department, known as Wings, said to me, 'Archie, did you happen to notice the hydraulic pressures?' All I could respond was, 'No, sir,' but in my head I was thinking, 'You've got to be joking! In those few seconds when I thought I was going to die, I wasn't immediately struck by the burning question, "I wonder what the hydraulic pressures are like?"'

The Board of Inquiry meeting was very tense; the maintenance side of aircraft in particular are always going to be concerned when there is an accident, because clearly something had happened that wasn't pilot error. This aircraft was out of control, and there were immediate suggestions that something had gone wrong on the technical side of the aircraft.

Unfortunately, it was never possible to make a technical examination because our helicopter only floated for a few minutes (one of the two flotation gears on the side had failed) and subsequently the rotation gear also detached and the aircraft sank in three thousand fathoms and was never recovered.

To tell the truth, though, we were elated by the whole thing, because nobody was killed; we thought it was a hoot. And it established our reputations: 'Those lucky bastards have got away with it,' which, ludicrous though it may seem to me now, thirty-five years later, at the time appeared to be quite glamorous, a real feather in your cap in military terms. Also, somebody said, 'Hey, you can be a Goldfish now.' I had never heard of it before, but we immediately wrote off to join, paid a five-pound subscription fee, and for that we got to join the Goldfish Club, and received a cool, rather understated little badge, which we sewed on to our overalls.

The accident had no psychological ramifications in terms of waking up at night, worrying about flying again or being stressed or afraid; in fact, we'd actually been scheduled to do night flying that evening and it was the worst conditions I had ever flown at sea. The only reason I stopped flying for the Navy was this road accident I had a few months later.

It was about seven o'clock on a sunny morning. I was in uniform, going to work at Yeovilton RNAS on my motorbike, when a chap drove straight out of his garage, didn't see me and just whacked straight into me. I fell off the bike and there was arterial blood pumping out over my head, and this chap took one look at that and ran away screaming. Fortunately, one of the first people to come along was a nurse, and she stopped the bleeding, and after that a petty officer medic from my squadron was passing and eventually I got hauled off to Yeovil District Hospital, and by about 10 or 11 a.m. I was in the ward.

The next morning – another sunny morning – I was lying in bed and wasn't in any pain; I was quite bored really. There was this big tent in the bed, but I thought, I'm not sure I'm quite ready to look at that yet, and I started listening to the radio. The local news came on: 'Somebody lost a leg last night in an accident . . .' and they read out my rank; they even had my name and address, which they also read out. I don't think that would be allowed now. And at that moment, it was, 'Well, Archie, what are you going to do now?' And I resolved that somehow I would go back to flying again. That was really all I wanted to do.

I spent the next few years getting over it. I went to Headley Court for a while, which takes months of work because you are a ragged mess of tissue and nerve endings and all sorts of things. In the end I was off flying for nearly four years.

But I got my commercial licence with the Civil Aviation Authority, who were very positive. I was quite impressed, because their attitude tended to be, well, why can't he fly? Instead of, why should we let him? So I got a commercial pilot's licence, then a transport pilot's licence, and I flew for about eight years on commercial aircraft in the North Sea, before starting on fixed-wing flying.

Commercial flying is a hard-bitten professional business, not the romantic thing that people might imagine; there's a famous poem about touching the face of God in the 'high untrespassed sanctity of space', and commercial flying is not like that at all. In fact, if I was dragging into Stansted or JFK through the usual turbulence and wind shear, the proximity of the face of God might be a source of alarm rather than comfort. But flying is my thing, and here I was recovering my vocation, and finding a sense of freedom, achievement and, above all, a sense of recovery, which was fantastic. And it was great to be flying again. For people like me, flying isn't just a job, it's a vocation.

My ambition after that accident was simply to recover normality and just get on with it. But of course the legacy of the
motorcycle accident remains, because there are certain issues of
pain that you can't escape.

I think what I realised is that when you are faced with these
immediate crises, when it appears you are about to die, there isn't
any seeing your life before your eyes in a kaleidoscopic or
chronological montage kind of thing. You just think: Fuck, this
is going to hurt . . .

JERRY ENGLISH

A rather fetching shade of green . . .

I went to Portsmouth for a Navy Day at the age of four, and there's a piece of film of me looking wistfully at this helicopter at the back of a ship, so even then I knew that would be the life for me. And that's what I did.

Not until I'd joined the Navy did I get to fly a little old Wasp; it was just around Dartmouth, but at incredibly low level, which was thrilling. A helicopter environment is essentially low-level; it's very rare for helicopters to be above one thousand feet, and for military helicopters above two hundred feet, because low-level is the safest place to be in hazard environment, where you have threats from an enemy. If I flew over your house at ten feet above roof-top level, you would hear me a split second before I arrived, and I'd be gone by the time you'd reached down to get your missile. If I were at ten thousand feet you would hear me about five minutes before I arrived, and have all that time to shoot me out of the sky with your heat-seeking missile, or whatever you had over your shoulder.

My first operational helicopter, in the seventies, was a Sea King, which was then relatively young in its career, and it was an exciting time because the Sea King was then pretty much state-of-the-art for anti-submarine work. Before that there'd been the piston-engine Whirlwind, where you could either carry a torpedo aimer, or a torpedo, but you didn't have enough power to carry both.

My first ditching occurred during my first few months on the squadron. I was on HMS *Tiger*, which had been used for the Smith Talks, when the then Prime Minister, Harold Wilson, and Ian Smith met up to discuss Rhodesia.

In 1974 we were doing an anti-submarine exercise in the Bay of Biscay, plus some deck-landing practice, and I was flying in a crew of four, with one American midshipman as a passenger who had never flown in a helicopter before. We were in between dips, where we landed our sonar body into the water from a forty-foot hover, and would then climb up to two hundred feet and transit to the next hover position.

We were at two hundred feet when the aircraft suddenly began to shake very violently, and it was clear there was something major wrong, although the engine indications were normal and there were no internal signs of anything wrong. But the controls were kicking around with the vibrations; in fact, they were so severe that the instruments, which were held in by friction screws, actually came out of the instrument panel. We tried various things, like switching the auto stabilisation off to see if that was interfering with the system, but nothing worked.

Another complication was that it became very difficult to talk to each other: in those days we wore throat mikes, which consisted of two microphones that went either side of your larynx, and because of the severity of the vibration they were actually bouncing clear of our throats, so our speech was very broken and hard to understand. The observer put out a Mayday call and I remember later hearing the tape of the call: 'We're g-o-ing to d-itch. M-m-mayday.' But, fortunately, the ship managed to work out there was something wrong with the helicopter and headed our way, and we turned into the wind, which is what you do to land a helicopter, and ditched it on to the sea; it would have taken only a few minutes to go from two hundred feet to actually landing on the water. The sea was about sea state 5, where you see white spume, and the waves were about six or seven feet high; it was December, but the Bay of Biscay is never terribly cold.

As soon as we landed on the water, we reduced the collective pitch on all the main rotor blades and the vibration almost ceased, so things became much calmer, and we could now actually talk to each other, so we stayed with the engines running and the rotors turning, although we could see that one of the blades was flying about a foot to eighteen inches lower than the other blades.

We were able to talk to the ship on UHF, and say we had what looked like a major blade problem, but that we were OK at the moment, and would try and get the aircraft on to the flight deck of the ship, because we thought we might be able to fly for a very short time, and it was worth the risk to save the aircraft, otherwise it would have sunk.

Having made that decision to land on the ship, they had to clear a space for us in the centre deck in double-quick time – and they jettisoned the captain's car, a Morris 1800, over the side of the ship, plus the squadron's Land Rover.

Unfortunately, just a few moments later, our tail rotor was hit by a wave and the aircraft began to yaw a little bit, then one of the flotation bags started to break away from the aircraft. We had a five-man dinghy in the back of the aircraft, and we all got in it, and at that point the flotation bag must have broken away completely, and the aircraft rolled over, floated upside down for a while and then sank.

The American midshipman who had been briefed on what would happen if we had an engine failure, or a ditching, turned to me in the dinghy as the aircraft was descending below the surface, and asked: 'This is an exercise, isn't it . . .?' Because everything happened exactly as we briefed it. 'No, this is actually happening for real . . . ' He went very white.

When you see your aircraft sink, you feel like a captain watching his ship go down, and then you think, 'Maybe we could have done something to save it . . .?' But, in hindsight, there was nothing we could have done.

We were winched up into one of the squadron's helicopters, and landed back on board, and everyone was very glad to see us back, except perhaps the captain who was fairly upset he had lost his car.

We'd had a Russian AGI, which was an intelligence gatherer trawler, a spy ship, bristling with aerials, following us. It was almost the first vessel on the scene, and in the end our lot dropped some depth charges in the area where our helicopter had sunk, just to put the Russians off, and to send a message: there's no reason now for you to trawl the sea depths . . . it was the Cold War, you see.

About a year later we were embarked on an exercise on HMS *Hermes* in the north Norwegian Sea, in the Arctic Circle. We were part of a trial for the development of a big helicopter carrier, and *Hermes* was the chosen trial vessel. We had been flying together as a crew for quite a lot of exercises, and we'd already had two fairly disastrous incidents that week, one with a fire in the air, although we managed to get the aircraft back and sort that out, and another one with a major instrument failure in the hover at night where we lost the sonar body, although we managed to get away with that too.

On this occasion, we got airborne on a filthy night, 17 November 1975. The wind was about thirty-five or forty knots, and it's never constant once it gets up that high, it's always gusting; there was a thirty-foot swell, and waves on top of the swell with the wind, and the temperature was about minus ten, the sea temperature was minus two, although that sea doesn't freeze because of its saline content, but it was very cold. Also, we had been briefed not only on the wind conditions but our survival times – I remember the Met man who gave the brief told us our survival time in the water was fifteen minutes.

So we were kitted up with all the warm layers: we had a set of long johns, and a long-sleeved white vest, then an Acrilan pile jumpsuit, which is called a bunny suit – in a rather fetching shade of green – and, finally, an immersion suit on top of that, which is a one-piece suit with rubber seals at the neck and the wrist, and rubber booties at the end of it.

The aircraft went unserviceable fairly quickly, so we landed back on the ship thinking that was us for that particular night. Unfortunately, they found another aircraft . . .

So we got airborne in that, and within fifteen to twenty minutes or so we were sitting in the hover, with a sonar body in the water, when there was an almighty explosion behind and above us in the area of the gearbox. We had an indication through the torque gauges that we'd had a torque split, and for some reason one of the engines had shut down. We discovered later that the shaft that drives into the gearbox had sheered. So we were then on one engine in the hover, and just about able to fly, but the first thing we did was to get rid of the sonar body, because that's a huge amount of weight, so we fired an explosive cable-cutter to cut the cable. We then attempted to get into forward flight, because in a helicopter the more forward air speed you have, the more lift you get. We managed to climb up to two hundred feet, and we were very pleased with ourselves because we could now fly back to the ship on one engine, and safely land the aircraft on the deck.

Unfortunately, the observer then informed us that hot oil was pouring out of the back, and the observer and the aircrewman were being covered in oil, which we couldn't see, because they were sitting in the dark, about fourteen to fifteen feet behind us.

We then got two more warning captions, which said *gear box oil low, oil pressure low*, and we looked at the gauge and it was on zero, and the aircraft was now starting to make terrible noises from the gearbox area, whining and graunching, and an even worse noise when the gearbox seized up as we came into the hover. I've never heard anything like that noise before or since; the sheer volume and intensity, just an agonising din.

So we then had to make a decision as to what we should do. The ship was not that far away, maybe four or five miles, but I said I thought we should ditch, with which everybody agreed, and so we then turned into the wind to ditch the aircraft. We knew it was going to be a nasty ditching, because we'd been down in the hover and seen how big the swells were.

As we came into a hover, the gearbox started to seize up again, and, once the blades start slowing down, the lift drops away because there's nothing to hold you up, plus we only had one engine anyway, and the aircraft just plummeted down into the sea.

We impacted at an angle to the swell, and the aircraft rolled over to the side. However, as soon as we impacted the first pilot, Graham Bell, decided he would release and get out of the helicopter, and as he released his harness the helicopter rolled violently to port, he fell across the cockpit and lost his window reference, which he needed to orientate himself. What you're supposed to do is wait for all motion to cease, and for things to stabilise, and then you release your harness and go out through your exit.

I waited as long as possible for things to stop moving, then I took a deep breath just before the water covered my mouth. The water was incredibly cold when it hit my face, really, really cold, which was a bit of a shock. And then I suddenly found Graham practically sitting on my lap trying to get out of the helicopter, but not knowing which way was up. He eventually got out through my exit before me, even though I hadn't had a chance to jettison the frame. How he got out through that tiny gap, I don't know.

Still underwater, and in the dark, I felt for my jettison handle, but noticed it was not where it should have been – with the impact the seat had actually compressed into the front compartment below me, so the handle was about seven or eight inches higher than it should have been. I eventually found it, and got out.

But all this activity was on just one breath of air. Graham had also taken out a lot of my airtime – I had words with him afterwards in a jocular fashion – and so I'd been underwater quite a long time by the time I got out. When I actually started swimming upwards, I remember thinking, this is taking a lot longer than it should do; perhaps the aircraft had sunk to the bottom, so there were around two thousand fathoms of water to the surface. And then I was sure I wasn't going to get to the top in time, I just wasn't going to make it. I was quite calm about it, but I had only been married a few months and I do remember thinking that it was a shame I wasn't going to have any children, and just feeling regret that it was all going to come to an end so soon. I was only twenty-one, quite young, and Carol had left the Wrens for me, because officers couldn't marry Wrens in those days, so she'd made a sacrifice in vain.

Anyway, I did reach the surface and began breathing, and got my dinghy off my back by releasing the harness and inflating it, and got into it. The observer and the crewman were near me, and I could see Graham a bit further away. The observer, a chap called Paul Collings, grabbed hold of my dinghy and tied the drogue cord on to his dinghy, and then he said to me, 'You'd better get your SARBE★ up, otherwise you won't get a tankard,' because, as he told me later, if you used your SARBE in a ditching situation, you got a free tankard from the manufacturers. I thought, considering our circumstances, that was a hilarious thing to have said.

We knew there was only one helicopter flying with a serviceable winch that night – and it was ours – and there were no other helicopters with a serviceable winch available to come and pick us up, which was not a nice thought at all. And, sure enough, a helicopter soon arrived overhead, but he couldn't do anything because he didn't have a winch, so he decided to mark our position by dropping a flare. What he didn't know, because all there was beneath him was inky blackness, was that our fuel tanks had ruptured so we were sitting in this huge pool of about four thousand pounds of av-cat (aviation-category) fuel, and the marker marine he'd dropped burns for an hour ... So we got out of there as best we could.

In the meantime the carrier had been closing on our position,

★Similar to a walkie-talkie.

and they had finally found an aircraft from the hangar down below decks that had a serviceable winch, but didn't have a serviceable Doppler, which tells you the movement of the aircraft over the sea. But they managed to get that airborne after about twenty-five or thirty minutes, and started to winch up Graham Bell: they went for the separated guy first, which was quite logical. We were all quite relieved he was being rescued, because the three of us together were a lot better off psychologically than he was on his own.

In fact, it was all quite jolly with us, although it was difficult to make conversation because the wind was very strong and howling, plus we were wearing helmets. You were supposed to take off your helmet and put the cape of the dinghy over you, but once you'd warmed your helmet up, the last thing you wanted to do was take it off in those very cold conditions. So we all kept our helmets on, and somehow we managed the usual naval banter, and made jokes about the bits of paper we were going to have to fill out for the inquiry, and to join the Goldfish Club when we got back, and so on.

Even if you're a very good sailor, the motion in a rubber dinghy on a sea of that size will make you feel sick. There were sea-sick pills on a line inside the dinghy, but the trouble was the tube had got a piece of tape around it and our hands had started to freeze up, despite our wearing cape leather gloves. So you try to open the tube of pills with your teeth, which is challenging, then you look inside and there's a piece of cotton wool stuck down in the tube, which is impossible to get at. So you learn that what works in a nice warm laboratory is not necessarily what works in a survival situation in the Arctic.

By this stage we'd reached well past our estimated survival time, so the captain of the ship asked for a volunteer seaboat crew, and the duty seaboat crew volunteered, led by a leading seaman. They launched this open whaler from the lee side of HMS *Hermes* to try to pick us up, which was a very brave thing to do in that sea, incredibly brave.

So while one helicopter was trying to pick up Graham Bell, which was taking quite a while, the seaboat was launched, and it came over to our position, which was being marked by another helicopter that was shining lights down at us, so the boat knew where to go. They reckoned they had one chance to pick us up, and try to turn round to get back to the ship, because turning an open boat in a huge swell like that, with waves on top, you're likely to get broached, and it only had a little diesel engine.

Actually, we had no idea they were coming until they were on top of us, because in a thirty-foot swell you don't actually see much at all unless you happen to come to the top of the swell at the same time as something else, which is what happened to us. Suddenly, a boat's bow appeared from the top of a wave, hands reached out and grabbed us – and dumped us in the bottom of this whaler. It all happened in a split second.

Everyone in the Navy has experience of handling boats, but not in those conditions, and we all knew how difficult it was going to be to get back. But they managed to turn this thing round, and headed back, and we came into the lee of *Hermes*, where it was still relatively rough. There's an interesting piece of equipment called Robinson's disengaging gear – which is good at releasing boats but a disaster for recovering them. Anyway, in theory it allowed the boat to be engaged simultaneously at both ends, and the intention was to connect to the uphauls that pull the boat up on to the cranes at the top. But we would get about six or ten feet above the waves, and then a big wave would come and smack the bow of the boat, and undo the disengaging gear at the bow, which meant we would drop back into the water at an angle of about forty-five degrees, just clinging on to the thwarts, the seats across the boat. They would then quickly lower the back end to get the boat level in the water, and attach it again, and then we would get smacked again. That happened three times, and it was actually one of the most frightening parts of the whole event – but eventually they managed to pull us up, and we got hauled up on to the ship.

There was a doctor who was temporarily serving on the ship, and he met us with a glass of brandy each, which was very morale-raising although probably not what he should have done, technically, and we were then taken down to sickbay. At that time, the treatment for exposure, from which we'd undoubtedly suffered, was to put you in a hot bath, which I do remember was excruciatingly painful, not initially, but when the feelings started to return.

Anyway, we were supposed to be kept in sickbay for twenty-four hours, when the last thing we wanted to do was sit in a bed and brood, but fortunately a raiding party from the wardroom came along and rescued us. They took us into the wardroom, barricaded the doors and got us very drunk, which I think was probably the best thing that could have happened.

We got flying again fairly shortly afterwards, although only Graham and myself continued flying as a career. I think the other two had had enough after that night.

I was very lucky to have survived that ditching. I'm glad it happened, though, because it was a testing time that I came through, and it just made me stronger, really. It also enabled me to understand how other people feel when they're in danger on the sea: twenty-three years of my life was in search and rescue, and I'd seen a lot of traumatic cases, and I could now empathise.

Having ditched twice I became known for it, and everyone was waiting for it to happen again. 'Hey, Jerry, when's going to be the third time?' people would ask. And aircrew would say, 'I'm not flying with you over that canal over there in case you ditch again!' But I didn't ditch again, and I've now hung up my flying boots, so I would hope, touch wood, there's not going to be another time.

STAN MARTIN

I'll die with my boots on . . .

My father had a factory in Brooklyn that made little girls'
coats, and my older brother worked with him; but when
America got involved in the war he went into the Service, and
I left school and went to work with my father – and hated

every day I had to be there. But I stayed there until I was called up.

I was initially drafted into the 66th Infantry Division, and I was just about finished with my basic training when my brother, who was in the aviation cadets, wrote to me and said, 'Get out of the infantry and get into the Air Force.'

Well, I've always listened to him, so I requested the papers from my sergeant, who was not too impressed, and transferred to the US Air Force. And a few weeks later they sent my old division over to France in two ships, and one of the ships was torpedoed and 750 men were killed.

They sent me to gunnery school in Texas; I had never been near an airplane, and my very first flight was a poor-weather day, but the pilot said, 'I'm going to take a chance, and take you up.' Well, I got into this airplane, an AT-6, and I had to pull a strap from the floor to hook on to my parachute, but I could hardly pick it up because the fellow before me had been airsick and it was kind of slimy.

Anyway, we went through the training, then we went to Lincoln, Nebraska, where we picked up a B-24, and flew to Syracuse, New York and from there to Bangor, Maine. We were en route to England when we discovered a gas leak in the plane, and had to divert to Iceland. When we arrived in Reykjavik, they couldn't fix the plane and the weather closed in, and my crew and I were stuck there for thirty days, and were confined to the base because the Icelanders didn't like us Americans. They felt we'd taken over their country with our Air Force bases. So that whole month we just hung around, ate a lot of doughnuts and played poker a lot. It was June, so it was daylight twenty-four hours a day, and it's quite a thing to not know day from night.

Eventually, we were put on a B–17 and flown to England, and the B–24 was left there and we became part of the 467 Heavy Bombardment Group, operating out of RAF Rackheath near Norwich.

March 4th, 1945 was a gorgeous day. We bombed Stuttgart. We encountered no planes, there was no flak and we dropped our bombs right on target; it was what we called a 'cream puff' flight, one of the easiest missions I'd ever been on. We used to call that a milk run. Everybody was very relaxed on the way home; there wasn't much talking. It just felt routine. None of us was expecting any trouble.

There were eight of us in formation. We were about four miles from the coast of England, heading for Rackheath, and so close to coming in to land we'd dropped back into a linear formation. I think ours was the last plane but one in the line, but I'm not sure because I was fast asleep at this point – I'd been up since 5.30 in the morning and I was exhausted. I was right near the escape hatch, when all of a sudden I heard somebody shout out, 'Help, we're hit!' Much later, I learned that the radio operator on my plane had neglected to put on the signal of the day, and when we came close to the coast of England, the British aircraft gunners didn't get the signal and shot us down.

I don't remember hearing any flak, but there was a mighty jolt, my head hit the ceiling, and all the ammunition fell on the floor, and I started to clear it up. I suddenly had this extraordinary energy but when I looked over at the rest of the crew, they were just standing there, frozen to the spot, their eyes popping out of their heads. I went to open the escape hatch, but I couldn't move it, and I was cursing them for not doing anything, and shouting:

'Give me a hand here.' But there was no movement at all from anyone. That image remained in my mind for quite some time: these men were just frozen in fear. Also, they didn't have their chutes on; maybe they weren't near them, I don't know, but everything was happening so fast, and now I wonder whether they just knew they didn't have time to make it out of the aircraft.

I pulled on the escape hatch and it finally opened, and a fellow, who had his back-chute on, fell out. Seeing him go, I thought we had finally got the order to bail out, so I hooked my parachute on to my chest and jumped out. I pulled the ripcord, and steered the chute away from the burning wreckage of our plane. When my feet touched the water, I threw my hands up and the chute flew away. I went under the water, pulled the cord on the Mae West and came to the top. I wanted to take my boots off, because they were so heavy, but every time I bent over to try and remove them, I drank a little seawater, so I thought, To hell with it, I'll die with my boots on.

I opened two packages of sea dye, and, fortunately, a civilian tanker, three storeys high, was coming by and saw it. Somehow this tanker managed to turn around and pull up right next to me. They put a ladder down, but I didn't have the strength to climb up it. So they sent two men down and pulled me up, laid me out on the deck, cut my clothes off me and put me in a bunk.

The first guy that fell out of our plane and I were the only ones to survive; the entire rest of the crew was killed. After the ditching, I was hyper, I couldn't walk any place, I had to run all the time, until they sent me to a place they called the Flak Shack, which was a rest home in Leicester for the American 8th Air Force. Oh, it was a fantastic place. I was there for ten days. I didn't want to go at first, I pleaded with them not to send me, and when my time was up I pleaded with them to let me stay. We were looked after there by lovely old gentlemen who couldn't do enough for us. They'd bring us freshly squeezed orange or grape-fruit juice in the morning – anything we wanted. And then there were four ladies, former Braniff Airways stewardesses, who would entertain us. They'd play cards with us, or we'd dance. In fact I was dancing with one of them when we got the news on the radio that President Roosevelt had died, and we stopped danc-ing then. It didn't seem proper.

Every one of us at the Flak Shack had been through some kind of trauma; we all knew that, and it would never be referred to. But there was one guy, a gunner, who spent all day, every day, in a bar nearby; it was obvious he was finished, his nerves were completely shattered. I asked one of the ladies what had hap-pened to him and it turned out that the first plane he ever flew in crashed on take-off and he was the sole survivor. And the same thing happened to his second plane, also killing everyone on board apart from him. He never flew again.

When I left the Flak Shack and got back to camp, there was a postcard from my mother, with a picture of an angel on it, wait-ing for me, which said: 'How are you? Is everything OK?' It was dated March 4th, the day I was shot down. When I came home to the States after the war, I said to my mother: 'You always sent me letters. How comes you sent me a postcard that day?' She said 'Oh, that night in my dreams *my* mother came to me and said: "Don't worry, I'm taking care of Stanley ..."' You know, it explains how I had time to get out of the plane. It was my angel, Grandma Bela, she was there. I still think of her all the time.

I was surprised how easily I returned to flying. It was partly because there was no choice. You just had to put these things behind you and get on with it, and I did a heap of missions after that.

When the war in Europe was over, I was reassigned to Boca Raton in Florida. When I got there, the sergeant major asked me what I wanted to do and I said: 'Nothing.' 'Well,' he said, 'I'll give you the next closest thing.' And I spent an hour a day marking cadets' papers. While I was there, a chaplain came to me and asked if I would mind speaking to the widow of one of the men from my plane, who wasn't convinced her husband was dead. That was painful; here was this lovely lady and I had to tell her that I knew her husband was not coming home. I tried to be as gentle as possible. I just let her know there was no way in the world he could have survived, without going into any detail. In some ways I think she was relieved. I didn't tell her about the radio operator forgetting to put the signal on. I didn't think she should know that.

I stayed in the Service until Japan gave up the fight and then I was released, and came back home to Brooklyn.

Having received a notice that I'd been in an accident, my father couldn't believe I wasn't injured and kept feeling my arms and legs. I arrived home Sunday at four o'clock in the morning, and at 8.30 a.m. on Monday I was in the factory. My brother and I had been away for four years, and for all those years my mother had been working with my father, and I didn't want that. So she was allowed to go home, and I went into the business, and I hated every minute of it. It was a terrible business: people would cut your heart out for penny.

When my father died in 1956, I closed the factory and took a job as an automobile salesman – I remember a Ford Mainline Tudor Sedan was the first car I sold, for $1200. Eventually I had my own dealership selling Fords, which really changed my life for the better.

Everybody tells me I'm doing very well, the doctors tell me I'm doing great – I just don't feel great, I feel eighty-eight years old, dammit. Your mind says 'go', but the body says 'no'. I hate to be negative, but I realise I shouldn't be making too many plans for the future. But one thing I can say is that every day since the ditching I've thought I was one lucky so-and-so to be alive.

Postscript

I regret to say that Stan Martin passed away at the end of 2011, just a few months after I had met him, in Hudson, New York, where he lived.

He had been cared for in the hospice ward at the Veterans' Administration Hospital in Albany, New York.

He was a charming and hospitable man, and I will always remember him.

He leaves two children, Pam and Eric.

ALLAN HURRELL

I'm quite a religious kind of bloke ...

I was living on a farm near Quellow, in Southern Rhodesia, when the war broke out; the local stationmaster told us the news, because we had no telephone on the farm. I was just about to start my last term of school, but as soon as I'd finished the

161

matric exam some friends and I went straight down to the recruiting office in Salisbury to join up.

I wanted to be a pilot, but I had to wait until November 1940, when the Empire Training Scheme was organised in Rhodesia. We trained on Tiger Moths at a place called Bulawayo, then we went on to twin-engine Airspeed Oxfords. When we'd completed that, we were seconded to Coastal Command in South Africa, where we did a navigation course, and from there we came across to the UK, where we were integrated with the Royal Air Force and issued with RAF kit. In the Rhodesian Air Force we wore bush shirts, short khaki trousers and long socks.

We were posted to Chivenor in Devon, where we were inspected by King George. Then up to Wick, in the north of Scotland, where we were sent out on various patrols as a strike force.

On 17 May, the German battle cruiser *Prinz Eugen* was heading towards the Baltic, and the whole of 86 Squadron went out to intercept this ship somewhere in the region of Stavanger in Norway to try and torpedo it. We turned south over the harbour. I was on the inside of the turn, so I was going a bit slower than some. I could see these 190s taking off, and there was also flak from the shore; you could see all these plumes of water going up. After we'd been going a little, this Focke-Wulf 190 came up from behind and attacked us. I could see tracer underneath me, and I got knocked out after a bit of shrapnel went through my chin and I lost consciousness.

Things got a bit confused after that.

When I came to we were flying at an angle, the sea was vertical and the aircraft was on fire – oh, it was hot as hell. I remember opening the hatch to get in a bit of air to try and cool things off. And then I conked out again. My navigator, Stuffy Collins, was trying to shake me awake; I can remember looking at him and noticing he had spots of red on his face, which was probably me breathing blood on to him. We weren't very high, we were only about a couple of hundred feet above the sea. I thought: We've got to get out of this thing . . .

As we landed on the water, I remembered to knock the parachute off me, the aircraft exploded and then I flaked out again. The next thing I remember I was in the water, and the aircraft was blazing all around me. I'm quite a religious kind of bloke, and I reckon He pulled me out of that aeroplane, I'm sure He did. I couldn't see any of the crew, and by now the aircraft had just disappeared. While I was in the water, the pilot who had shot me down flew over and I put my hand up so he could see I was still alive and he could arrange for me to be picked up. We rescued their chaps as well, you know: any German aircraft shot down in the Channel were picked up by the RAF, or air-sea rescue.

I must have been in the water for quite a number of hours.

Before we took off for the flight, somebody had swiped my Mae West from my locker. There was an old Mae West lying in the corner, all dirty and oily. I put it on because it was the only one there, but I remember feeling it and thinking: It hasn't even got a compressed-air bottle. Anyway, when I hit the sea I thought: Well, I'd better blow this Mae West up. But I couldn't blow it up because my jaw was cracked and hanging down, I couldn't make any pressure. So I closed off the tube. But while I was lying there I saw this petrol tank from the aircraft, so I hopped on to it. And, as I was climbing up, the little lever for the compressed air turned on by itself – that's another reason I reckon Jesus was with me – and suddenly the Mae West blew up and I dropped back into the water, and just flaked out again, and I was out until I woke up in hospital.

I could hear all these people talking and I remember thinking, why are all these Matabele here? I thought I was in Africa. And how the heck have I got here? But eventually I realised these people were speaking German, and I was in hospital. Anyway, they stitched me up, and this German bloke who had come out to rescue me spoke English, and said they'd picked me up and put me on a Norwegian boat, which they'd commandeered. According to this chap, I began struggling, and in the mêlée somebody knocked over a paraffin lamp and the boat caught alight, and they were all pitched overboard and had to tread water. Why they didn't just push me under I don't know, because they must have been pretty fed up with me. Anyway, they sent out a German seaplane to pick me up.

One of the tragedies is that the rest of my crew didn't survive. The navigator, Stuffy Collins, was alive before we hit the deck, I know that, but I didn't see him again. I didn't see any of them again, actually. They were all good blokes.

I was in a ward for nearly twelve weeks, along with a German bloke who'd fractured both his legs. The Norwegian nurses were very good to me, and I had to go with an escort to the dentist in town to have my jaw set again.

One of the nurses was in the Resistance, and she asked if I'd like to escape. She said she could arrange my escape to Sweden. I thought about it, then I asked her: 'What would happen to the nurses here?' She said they'd probably be punished in some way or another, so I said: 'Look, it's not worth it for all these lovely people.'

Inevitably, once I'd healed my time came to be taken to Germany. First of all, I was taken by rail from Stavanger to Oslo, where I spent the night in the Gestapo headquarters. A bloke there tried to get information from me; he wanted to know where I'd been and why. But I had nothing new to tell him. From there I was escorted to Copenhagen by a guard, from Copenhagen it was on by train to Frankfurt-on-Oder, and from there we went to Stalag 344, not far from Breslau. The German Air Force camps were full, so we were put in this big Army camp, which held about fourteen thousand British troops, mostly lower ranks. Under the Geneva Convention they could be sent out to work, and went on working parties to different places, but because we Royal Air Force blokes were considered a bit stroppy, we were in a camp within a camp, and weren't allowed out, and couldn't move out into the Army blokes' area, so we just used to see them across the fence. I was there for nearly three years.

I met a very amusing bloke called Phil Bridgeman who became a great friend, probably my best friend ever. He was a Canadian navigator flying Wimpys, and he had been shot down over Germany on his very first operation, which really annoyed him. Another thing that annoyed him was that I'd got a war scar, and he had nothing. He really wished he had a scar somewhere! Anyway, after we'd been there a year or so, he and I had decided we'd try to escape by joining one of the working parties. The only way you could do that was to swap identities with an Army bloke, so I swapped identities with a chap called Bailey, while he took my place in the Air Force camp. I had to learn his number, his father's and mother's name, all those sort of personal things. And then we went out on a working party. I'd only been out a few hours when I was suddenly called back to the camp and marched before the Krieg officer, who wanted to know why I'd put a German girl 'in the family way'. Apparently Bailey had met this girl on a working party and they'd had relations. He'd thought she was Polish, but she wasn't, and he ended up going to court because she was German – they were very strict about that sort of thing. So I went back and got hold of Bailey and we changed back pretty quick. They really hammered that poor girl; she was sent to prison. I never contacted or saw Bailey again after that, but I often wondered whether he ever did the right thing after the war, and went to get her and their child.

There then followed a period where the Germans tied us up during the day. The Jerries decided that, because we didn't go to work, they couldn't keep an eye on us, so all of us in the Air Force had to be tied up. So they tied us up with Red Cross string in the morning, and we'd go around all day like that, which was a bit difficult when you had to go to the loo ... Anyway, that went on for a bit, and then they decided to use handcuffs. Every evening they'd count all the handcuffs, and maybe they'd be one short, so they'd count them all again and then they'd be two short. The German officers would get pretty hectic, shouting and waving, and pointing guns and things. 'Produce these handcuffs!' So they'd count them all again, and now they'd have two or three extra. We really messed them around. Eventually they packed it up.

The Red Cross parcels were very erratic. At one stage we'd get them once a week, then it became once a month, and in the end it was only now and again. Actually, if it weren't for the Red Cross we would have had our chips, I reckon. The Germans used to give us mint tea in the morning, which nobody drank; we just used it for shaving, because that was our only hot water. Later on in the day you had a ration of potatoes and soup and a loaf of bread. Everybody was hungry. In the barracks you shared a table with ten blokes, and each week one bloke would be called the Ration King, and he'd dole out the food. When the potatoes came he'd put them out in ten little rows, and he'd cut the loaf into ten pieces, then there was a pack of cards, with ten names on, and you'd shuffle them, another bloke would cut them and put the numbered cards against the food. This was so there was no favouritism at all, and everyone got the same amount of food.

A lot of people played cards. I played a lot of bridge and my partner was an American chap in our barracks, who was a baseball professional. We must have been quite good because we won quite a few tournaments. We used cigarettes as chips, because no one had money, of course, and the winner took all the cigarettes, although we didn't actually smoke them, as they were a form of currency in the camp.

I did try to grow a few vegetables on a little piece of ground near the latrine, and I grew a beautiful marrow, but just as I was ready to pick it somebody swiped it for their dinner.

I endlessly walked around the perimeter, and read, and wrote: we were allowed to send one letter a month. I'd met a girl in England called Doreen Hepworth. We were more or less committed to each other by the time I was a prisoner of war. I wrote to Doreen in England, and told her I was hoping to become a veterinary surgeon, and asked if she could send me some books and she sent me a veterinary dictionary, and biology and zoology books, and I did quite a lot of studying in my spare time. A New Zealander who'd trained as a vet in the United States used to give talks, and I'd go and chat to him quite a bit.

Some British dentists had been captured, and there was a sort of clinic in the hospital, although you had to wait nearly a year if you wanted a filling, so it was best just to have the tooth pulled out. I'd lost eight teeth when I was shot down, and I had no top teeth on one side. The scheme was, you pitched up at the dental place on a certain day; you'd find about ten or twelve blokes there already waiting. The orderly would come along and say: 'Which tooth is it?' And you'd say: 'This one here.' So he'd put 'molar number three' against your name, then when your name was called you'd get in the chair and the dentist would extract a tooth in half a minute. That was quite an experience.

In January 1945 the Russians were advancing into Germany. The Germans decided we had to go west, as they were afraid of what the Russians would do to them. We marched from Lansdorf right through to a place called Ziegenhain, which was not far from Dresden. We marched five hundred miles in the bitter cold – 1945 was one of the worst winters for a long time. There must have been a thousand of us in this group, and we'd march during the day, then stop and camp either out in a field or on a farm. Some places had barns where we could at least get some straw to lie on, but usually we were out in the open. We spent a few days at another prisoner-of-war camp, and then we marched on again, but when we got to the next place, a camp called Zeigenhain, all the Germans suddenly pushed off. They said if we wanted to come with them we could. We said: 'No way, bye-bye Charlie.' Soon after that, Patton's tanks arrived. They came zooming into the camp, and didn't even stop: they just threw rations to us from their jeeps, which we consumed pretty quickly.

While we were in that camp we discovered a whole lot of parcels belonging to the French prisoners, which had never been dished out, so we sort of commandeered them. A lot of these parcels had food in them, but it must have gone rotten because we all got diarrhoea and I spent most of my time on the loo. And while I was on the loo, some swine pinched my blanket; I had a nice thick blanket, which had been sent to me from my parents via Rhodesia House. Gone.

Anyway, soon after that the British Army arrived and we were taken to an airfield where a whole heap of Dakotas were landing, and from there we flew to England, and that was the end of my life as a POW.

When I arrived in England, I was given double rations and sent off on leave, so I went to find Doreen. She'd joined the WAAFs when I was shot down, and become a fitter. I went to the address I had for her in Bingley, Yorkshire, but it was empty, there was nobody in the house. I was standing there, wondering what to do, and a neighbour said: 'They've gone to Weston-Super-Mare.' Oh, OK. So I took the train and eventually got to Weston-Super-Mare, and I heard she was working in Bristol, where her parents had a factory which made piston rings. So I went to Bristol, and I was walking along the street with my kitbag on my shoulder, looking for this office, when suddenly somebody tapped me on the shoulder, and said: 'Ee lad, you've come home.' It was

Doreen's father, who was a real Yorkshireman. He had an accent you could cut with a knife. Anyway, I stayed with them for a bit, and Doreen and I got married on 27 April 1945 with my Canadian friend, Phil Bridgeman, as best man.

The Rhodesian government gave me £120 in bonds, and a grant and a loan of £150, so I could go to university. You had to pay back the loan, which I did, fifteen years after I qualified as a vet, and Doreen and I eventually got a house in Edinburgh.

I turned ninety in September last year. I feel quite honoured really to have reached this age, because pretty well all my friends have passed on, apart from Phil Bridgeman, although I'm a bit worried because I haven't heard from him for a couple of months or more.

The best thing is having a very supportive family – I have two children, nine grandchildren and two great-grandchildren now. I'm not quite as brisk as I used to be, and I'm very deaf. After Doreen died I decided to join the Goldfish Club. It is quite exclusive, isn't it? There aren't many of us Second World War people around, and it's wonderful to share these experiences.

BAILLIE NOBLE

I never did care for water . . .

At the beginning of the war I served on a minesweeper in the Royal Navy, stooging up and down the Hull estuary looking for magnetic mines, which was blooming monotonous. So I applied for transfer to the Fleet Air Arm, and I was sent to St Vincent, a training college for potential flyers in Portsmouth. I arrived in January '41, at the height of the Blitz, when there were raids on Portsmouth every night. The hostel we were booked into went up in flames and we spent hours helping the wounded and getting elderly folk into shelters. When I tried to get back into the hostel to retrieve my papers, a CPO tried to stop us entering. We pushed him off, and left him cursing and threatening to report us as 'assaulters and defaulters'. However, the next day we heard that the poor fellow had been killed in the raid. Death was everywhere.

We did our elementary flying on Magister and Master two-seater monoplanes, then trained as fighter pilots on Fulmars and Sea Hurricanes. The Sea Hurricane was the one I really loved. I was posted to the Elite 809 fighter squadron – and then I made it up Scapa Flow to join the aircraft carrier HMS *Victorious*, and that was my first experience of landing on a carrier. I did all right, I think, but talk about going in at the deep end!

In July 1942 we sailed from the Orkneys to escort the August Malta convoy. We entered the Med in convoy, at night, and we had a lot of harassment from German Heinkels based on the island of Pantelleria. It was a terrible business. Our navy was bombed and sunk continuously; three thousand men were lost and only two vessels out of seventy-five reached Malta. I did a BB attack on three Heinkels and shot down one which made the basic mistake of turning away, so the gunner couldn't get a sight on me. But, actually, those planes had a terrific firing range; in fact, if the Germans had had more Heinkels I'm sure they would have won the war. I fired some more rounds into the other Jerries, but had to break off because I hadn't got too much fuel left.

My next mission was to cover the North Africa landings; I flew a Fulmar this time and took an observer, Lorimer Rothermere, with me, who took photographs of the hill fort at

Aumale, a few miles from Blida, the HQ of some very vicious and cut-throat Arabs. There was talk that one of our fighter boys had been captured after being knocked down by anti-aircraft fire and was being held to ransom there. Anyway, they were certainly knocking down any aircraft which came within range, and I suppose I was flying a bit low, and the blighters began firing some kind of cannon gun and hit us twice. Heading back towards the ship, I realised the fuel gauge was almost at zero, so I decided to ditch in the drink rather than have my engine cut out. I told Lori, 'We are going to have to ditch.' He was all right about it; well, I suppose he didn't have much of a say as I was the pilot.

Not being able to swim, I aimed for what I thought was the beach, but because we were zigzagging we ended up about fifteen miles from the coast. I kept the stick up, so she landed at an angle. It couldn't have been a better landing on water, so we didn't turn upside down, thank goodness . . . I only wish more people had seen it! When your aircraft starts going down, you've got so much to do, and your mind is racing so fast you haven't time to be frightened.

But my harness must have broken; I was knocked against the reflector sight and broke my jaw and was out for quite some time. When I finally got out of the cockpit, I stood on the wing, which was already underwater, trying to get some air into my Mae West, which is always left deflated because if you were to land in water with one fully inflated the impact would break your neck. But I couldn't blow it up because I'd also broken all my teeth on the reflector sight and a lot of very persistent blood kept getting in the way. There was no sign of the rubber dinghy, which should have ejected on impact and self-inflated. It was a blooming good thing Lori could swim. At that moment I sure wished I had learned to swim. I should have been able to swim but I never did care for water.

Of course, eventually I ended up in the water and I watched the plane disappear from beneath me, and sink eight hundred feet to the bottom of the sea.

Lori was a good swimmer, while I was just splashing about doing doggy paddle and swallowing a lot of water, although fortunately it was September so the water was quite warm.

It seemed we were there for a heck of a long time, but it was probably not much more than an hour later when the sharp bow of the destroyer HMS *Quiberon* appeared, and we climbed up scramble nets to the deck. The *Quiberon* was a Royal Australian Navy ship with an English captain; Browning, I think his name was. The poor chap had more or less lived on the bridge for the past ten days, watching out for U-boats, and he was a very brave man, because he rescued us despite orders not to stop in U-boat-infested waters. No captain likes to be a sitting target.

I hadn't felt much pain in the water, but once I was on the ship I realised I wasn't in a very good way. I also had a spinal injury, and two or three days later I was transferred from *Quiberon* to HMS *Victorious* by bosun's chair, while the two ships were refuelling and travelling at some fifteen knots.

There was no particular celebration in the mess when I got back – this sort of thing was a pretty ordinary happening – you just had to get stuck in again. Except I didn't, because after I ditched I couldn't fly. That drop in the Med not only messed up my back and my eyes, it put an end to any chance of promotion. There I was thinking I'd end up with my own squadron, and it turned out to be the end of my Fleet Air Arm career, despite all my letters and pleas to the Admiralty to let me return to my squadron.

Instead I was sent to train as a radar control director, directing aircraft off the carrier, which was a painful job to have when you really wanted to fly. I'd qualified as an architect before the war, and after the war I went back to it, and that's how I spent my working life. I've reached my hundredth birthday – which is quite an achievement – but not the one I wanted, because I never did fly again.

DENNIS McCAIG

Who should arrive, but the SS . . .

I was born in Fiji, where my father was a district officer. In those days, Fiji was a remote Crown Colony with a great depth of loyalty to the mother country; we supported King and Empire, and all that. But the only time we really connected with the outside world was through *London Calling* on the World Service at six o'clock each evening. I was fascinated by the news. The Germans were advancing through France and Belgium, and they were beating hell out of us, and I thought: I've got to get there . . . The heroism of the Battle of Britain fighter pilots meant they were the centre of attraction, and I wanted to be one.

Then we heard they were calling for volunteers from the Dominions and the Colonies, and I applied for the RAF, but terrified I might not make the grade. There was a long delay of something like three or four months before they said, 'OK, you're selected.' We were scheduled to leave on a boat, on 1 April

1941; we were called the First Fiji Contingent. There were nineteen of us, all ages and backgrounds, but all white, of course.

I'd been at boarding school, but this was my first real parting from home, and there was a lot of sadness about it. When we made our farewells, people stuck pound notes into our shirts as a contribution, and I got around thirty pounds, which in those days was a great deal of money. A passenger ship took us to New Zealand, and there we had to wait in barracks some weeks for the onward trip to Sydney, and then something like three months for the next trip around Australia to Perth, and then we joined the Rhodesian Air Training Group, flying Tiger Moths, and then on to Harvards – advanced stuff. I'd never been in a plane before, and it was a wonderful experience; when I went up into the air I felt the world was mine. I was eighteen or nineteen when I got my wings, and full of the exuberance of youth.

After training we had a two-day journey by train to Cape Town, where we waited for a troopship to take us to Liverpool, taking a circuitous route across the Atlantic because of the submarine threat. Liverpool in wartime winter was ghastly. It was wet, cold and foggy, and we didn't know what the hell was going to happen to us. Then we had an overnight train trip to the Personnel Dispatch Centre at Bournemouth, which was crawling with recently trained aircrew, and we languished there, and got into trouble. We didn't have much money, just enough to get a little bit pissed, and then one night out we collected signs from all around the town, amassing a very good collection, until the police arrested us. The gardens in Bournemouth at the time were enmeshed in barbed wire and they put us in a compound there. We decided we'd have to make a bolt for it, which we did, and we got away. I don't say I am very proud of that episode. It was just boredom; we were young chaps, doing nothing, and nothing to do.

We were then posted up to Dundee in Scotland to fly the magnificent Hurricane. Huge and intimidating after what we'd been flying, it was like driving an omnibus after a Mini Minor. That plane was a battleship, and it had eight guns on it, four of them machine guns, .303s on each side, and of course it had a reputation from the Battle of Britain. It was marvellous to fly. And we had to learn how to fight with it: we had to do formation flying, battle manoeuvres and firing the guns at flying targets towed by Lysanders. I was good at that. If you scored over a certain number of hits you had the bottom half of your black tie cut off and pinned on the board, and I had to spend a fortune on new ties.

I was then sent off to Air Gunnery Training school, which was the last step before becoming a pilot. But at that time there were too many pilots coming through and not enough getting killed, so there was a bottleneck. So instead of joining a fighter squadron with all its glory, I went off as a staff pilot to Number 10 Air Gunnery School at Barrow-in-Furness, which was, to put it crudely, the arsehole of the world (although I'm sure it's very nice nowadays). That was a very unhappy period. I wrote to the Governor of Fiji and the Colonial Office to get me the hell out of there. But there was a roster, and gradually those on top were posted to operations, and then one day we were posted to Spitfires, and of course that really was the dream world.

We then assumed we were days away from the squadron, but we weren't; we were days away from going to Blackpool, and from there to the Middle East, where we languished in a ghastly camp in Tripoli, and then finally a postings corporal posted me to 249 Squadron, based in Termoli on the Adriatic coast of southern Italy. 249 Squadron was part of the Balkan Air Force, set up to help partisans across the water; it hadn't just got Spitfires, but its own bombers too.

All our work was ground-based: dive-bombing, strafing, and of course it was dangerous. The Germans had no fighting aircraft over that area, but they had a great deal of flak, and when you went out on operations the ground flak was intense.

My first op, we dive-bombed a German army depot. You turned the aircraft and went down virtually vertically, released two bombs, and then zoomed up, just hoping the flak was not going to hit you because it was coming all the time. Then you rejoined and went looking for locomotives or MT (military transport), basically anything moving on the ground. We came across a truck and a German staff car, and we strafed them, and that was thrilling, going down and frightening the daylights out of the poor occupants of the car, and we destroyed that target, zoomed up and headed home.

It was exciting while you were doing that sort of thing, exhilarating even. But when you were on the ground, waiting two or three days for decent weather, or suitable targets dreamed up by somebody far away, it was boring. We were parked in tents stuck out in the open, and it was a very rough life, hot and dusty in summer, freezing in winter, and the food was bloody awful, almost beyond description.

We then converted to Mustangs: this wonderful new American aircraft where everything was gleaming and sparkling compared to the tired old Spitfires that had been through the desert war. Also, they had a better range, so we could do long-range patrols right down into Greece, just looking for chance targets. We found two Focke-Wulf 190s on a German airfield, about an hour's flight from the base, and strafed them, and that was wonderful, until we discovered that flak had penetrated my radiator. My no. 1 said to me: 'You know you are streaming white?' which meant that glycol, the coolant, was drifting out, and when it's gone there's nothing to lubricate the propeller, so my engine was going to pack up, which it did, and I bailed out at about ten thousand feet into the Greek mountains.

I'd been on a dawn reconnaissance, so it was still light, but descending in a parachute was terrifying. Eventually, I hit the ground. I was shocked and exhausted by this time, and there I stayed for a long while, with not another human being for miles around me, it would appear; it was so remote, there weren't even any roads. Eventually some children found me and brought me to their village.

It was more primitive than anything I'd ever witnessed, including the Fiji villages, and there was real poverty. But the inhabitants were delighted to see me because they were partisans, and they hid me for a week or more until an escort from partisan headquarters came for me. We set out at dawn, walking over the mountains, with just grapes and dry bread to eat, and late that same evening we arrived at the partisan camp, where we were met by an American who was attached to the partisans. 'We must get down the mountain right away,' he said, although by this time it was raining, it was dark and I was tired and hungry. He took me down this very steep mountain on the back of a donkey, which was murderous, and by the time I got down to the village eight hours later I was practically locked on to the back of that donkey, and couldn't stand up.

I stayed there for about two weeks, and became the chief adviser to the building of an airstrip – if you could call it an airstrip: it was more a rough piece of ground. It was here that I encountered the glory of ticks. I'd been given a house where I was bitten in lines along my body by these bloody ticks, because the hygiene was so awful. Eventually, we managed to create a rough surface for the length of a thousand yards, and some Dakotas came in at night-time, and I was taken out to a rest camp in Capri. Great food and a beautiful location, but I just wanted to get back to my squadron.

When I did get back to Termoli, I found about half the other guys were gone. The shot rate was quite high. But we were very callous about people getting the chop. If Jim had had a decent camera or something, it was: 'OK, who is going to have old Jim's camera?' I acquired a new gun like that, a .32 automatic, which was a great improvement on the tired old six pistol thing I had before.

German E-boats were reported to be in this part of the Adriatic, and we were sent out to recce the place to see whether that was true. We spotted these E-boats tied up in Fiume harbour, and we thought: 'Just one high-powered rush down in a steep dive run with all engines open, set the bead on the E-boat, press the gun button, strafe them, and zoom away. That's all we'll have to do.' Unfortunately, I flew into a line of flak and was hit. This time I bailed out into the sea. And that was murderous.

On my way down I saw my Mustang hit the sea, and then I hit

the water shortly afterwards. I went down and down, and the parachute dropped on top of me and very nearly drowned me. I was struggling to get out from under it, encumbered with flying boots and heavy clothes. Eventually I extricated myself from underneath the canopy and got into my dinghy. But I couldn't stay in the sea, it was freezing; I had to make for the islands, which were visible within a mile or so. However, before I got to the islands I could see all these guys down on the shore, and I could see they were in uniform, but I couldn't tell what type. In fact, as I got closer, I could see they were in German uniform, although, as it turned out, they were Italians. They pulled me out of my dinghy, gesticulating and jabbering, with me not being able to speak Italian, and them not being able to speak English. But I did eventually discover they were forced labour, working for the Germans, and having reckoned I would be rescued they wanted me to take them, all nine of them, as my prisoners of war.

Eventually, a Catalina, answering my Mayday call, arrived; it flew in a circle, orbiting over me, escorted by two Spitfire 9s and a Mustang, so there was plenty of fire power there. They then started flashing orders: they wanted me to swim out two hundred yards, where the Catalina would pick me up. But when I told the Italians this, they said: 'Not on your bloody nelly.' They wanted the craft to come in to the shore, so we would all get on board. Discussions reached stalemate, and the Spitfires and the Mustang flew off and the Italians took me up to their huts on the plateau and gave me something to eat, and some ouzo to drink, where-upon I passed out.

In the middle of the night, who should arrive but the SS. I'd been betrayed to the Germans, who pushed me around and roughed me up. And that's where I ended my war and became a German prisoner of war. I was put in a dungeon, which had graphics of little figures hanging from gallows on the walls, etched by other prisoners who'd been incarcerated there.

On the long and very tedious journey to Germany in a convoy and on trains, we were dive-bombed and strafed by our own people on four occasions. It was just a matter of having good enough luck to survive. The convoy was laden with goodies they had robbed from the Italians, and I was at the back of this truck all on my own with a canopy over the top. When we were bombed one night I jumped out of the truck and got into a little tunnel underneath the road – which turned out to be full of German soldiers, so I got back into the convoy. We went on to some place where I had my first food for a day and a half, at a soup kitchen where these German civilians discovered I was on the British side. They began throwing stones at me and shouting and swearing, because they'd just been bombed. But I was escorted by this very pleasant German warrant officer, who said: 'We've got to go round the town now, because if we go through it they might murder you.'

A farmer's wife picked us up at the side of the road, took us home to her farm and gave us a really good meal, which was marvellous. I'll always remember her kindness, which seemed a rare commodity at that time. Well, she was a mum, is the way I'd put it. And then we went on, and after a very long and tiring walk we picked up the railway on the other side of town and eventually got to Nuremberg, having been strafed twice on the way.

At Nuremberg we were dispersed to a POW centre and given

clothes and a meal, and went from there to the interrogation centre, which was a shock because I was locked in a room on my own: no sound, no lights; the only communication was when someone slid a plate of food underneath the door. Eventually I was interrogated by a young German chap, but I had little or nothing to tell him, and from there I was sent off to the main camp in Nuremberg, which was a huge ants' nest of POWs of all nations.

The Americans were all over Europe during that time. It was only a couple of months before the end of the war now, and we could hear General Patton's army advancing; we could hear their guns. Eventually the Germans decided we would make decent hostages and they planned to march us towards Munich rather than let us go free. So we were assembled into this huge column of human beings, with dogs and guards alongside us, and we walked through open country. It was February, snow was on the ground and there was no food other than an occasional sack of potatoes we managed to find in a farmer's field.

Eventually my feet gave out. I had huge blood blisters and I said to the chap I was walking with: 'I can't go any further, I'll just have to stop here and take my chances.'

It was during that stage we were strafed by US Air Force Thunderbolts: they dive-bombed the railway station, which was nearby, and then they strafed us. You could hear the bullets pinging. They killed a lot of people in our convoy, which was absolutely terrifying. We carried on, and at the next stop there was a little stream where I was able to prick all my blood blisters and drain them. Sitting there waiting for the word to go on, we got news there were Red Cross parcel trucks at the next stop, and that was sufficient incentive for me to carry on. The parcels had everything: cigarettes, of course, biscuits, tins of stew, soap, and they were an absolute godsend because they kept us going until we reached a huge camp called Mussberg 7A*. It was crowded there: you could hardly lie down in your hut. But the English had control, and after three or four days we could hear the squealing of tanks on the reaches above us and then we were liberated.

After I was demobbed I went back to Fiji; my father was in a position of some influence and got me a job. But I couldn't settle down, and for a long time after the war I suffered from depression, post-traumatic stress disorder they call it now, although the term wasn't familiar at that time. I'd got married by then, and went through a very rough time with my marriage, and eventually my wife left me. She couldn't stand it out in Fiji, or me.

I'm not qualified to say what caused my depression. I just think these wartime experiences were terrible. Ditching is just a word, but actually it is awful to do. Also, walking 180 miles in the open, in winter, with virtually no food, took a lot out of everybody. But the whole world was at war, and everybody suffered casualties, except Fiji, which had only been on the perimeter of the war, and when I got home no one was interested in me or what I had been through.

I waited until I could save up sufficient money and then came back to England, and rejoined the Royal Air Force. I went from the wartime propeller-driven planes into jets, and several different types of jets. I loved flying, it was a great part of my life. But in the end it got too complicated for me, and I was happy to leave at forty-three. I think I was just worn out.

I married again and had a very successful second marriage and two lovely children, so I've got two families. I have most things of material comfort now: I've got a nice place to live, all on my own, I've got a car, I have a few friends, although they are dying off; and I have loneliness. I'll be ninety this year, and sometimes I think I'm very lucky to be alive, but there are times when I think I've lived too long.

KEVIN TOPHAM

Worse odds than the Titanic, *wasn't it . . . ?*

The country was bankrupt in 1965, like it is now, and the government wanted all trained drilling crews on the North Sea, looking for gas. I worked on the first rig, which was called the *Sea Gem*, and it was built in sections on the docks in Middlesbrough, then towed out to Dogger Bank. We started drilling, 'spudding in', as they call it, on Parcel 48, a section of the North Sea about forty minutes by chopper from Immingham, on the Lincolnshire coast, and in October of that year we struck the first North Sea gas well.

I was 'derrickman', which meant when we were changing the drill bit I would be working on the top. I'd climb up a ladder about two or three hundred feet high, pull twelve thousand feet of drill pipe out, and, using huge powered spanners, break it all off in ninety-foot lengths, then stand them on the derrick floor. It used to take us about eight hours or so to put a new bit on.

The accommodation block was dead under the chopper deck, so on nightshift you could hear the choppers come down with a thump when you were trying to sleep, but you got used to it. And actually, our quarters were brilliant. We had a cinema, which got all the new films straight from London, and each man had a steward, who did your beds and brought you out trays of stuff on nightshift. When I got home, I told my wife each one of us had a steward on the rig, and she said: 'Well, you haven't got one now, get washing up!' We worked twelve-hour days: ten days on, seven till seven, then five days off, but if it was foggy you didn't get off because the choppers wouldn't fly in fog.

The *Sea Gem* collapsed on Boxing Day, of all days. On Boxing Day morning they called me at home to say they needed me, and sent a taxi to my door to take me to Immingham, where I caught the chopper at about 2.15. We had a slap-up Christmas dinner on the rig, the wife of the BP chairman had made a big cake in the shape of the drilling rig, so we had some of that, and then, as I was going to be on nightshift, I went up to my bunk for a bit of a read and a sleep. Suddenly, two of the two-hundred-foot steel back legs collapsed. At first I thought they were being lowered in preparation for moving – we'd already capped the well off because we were preparing to move to another site not far away – but they went down way too sudden, so I figured something was wrong straight away.

The radio cabin was the first thing that went into the sea, so we then had no Mayday at all.

I went out on to the deck. It was a grey December day – well, the North Sea is always grey – and it was just a disaster. The two-hundred-foot derrick was floating, some of the legs were breaking off, some were floating about, and others just sinking, and I thought: 'God, how are we going to get out of this?' I'd been in some tight spots during the war, but this was really a tricky one. All we had was one lifeboat, but it was floating away. To this day, my abiding memory of that day was seeing our lifeboat drifting away, with nobody in it. That was the worst thing of all.

There was only a skeleton crew on board at that time of year, but still, one lifeboat for thirty-nine men? Worse odds than the *Titanic*, wasn't it?

We did have some Carley floats, which are a kind of inflatable dinghy: you sling them over the side, pull the cord and they inflate. The first one we pulled inflated, but as the rig sank lower a wave came over and flung the dinghy, which we hadn't tethered, back at us. So we lost that one. We then had to walk along the handrail, which was like walking on a tightrope under water, to get to the next one. We did manage to get that dinghy going, and we tethered it to the handrail, and got about fifteen men off on that, including me. One guy cut the rope, and we just floated away with two little paddles. Then we spotted the fitter, who was hanging over the rail with a fractured skull and broken ribs; he was a real mess. So we decided to paddle back and get him off, although by now all the heavy stuff was crashing off the rig and sliding down, pipes and enormous big pumps were falling into the water, barrels of fuel oil were tumbling down, and the huge crane almost crashed on top of us. A few more feet and it would have taken us down.

Our float was in a hell of a state, you can't imagine what was in there with us: vomited-up Christmas dinners, blood, and God knows what. The waves were slopping over the sides, these things were really not fit for twenty-foot waves in the North Sea, plus we were overloaded. We were bailing everything out with a helmet and gumboots. I was reasonably OK, but I'd got knocked about a bit before getting into the dinghy, which had come back and hit me, and it bruised the whole of my right leg. I still feel it now, occasionally. Also, I was freezing, we all were, because we had no survival suits. I mean, I was in pullover and slippers, and shirt and trousers. It was fortunate we were all young blokes, and pretty fit. I was thirty-seven years old, and in those days I played football and all that. I'm eighty-three now, and I don't think I would last so well these days.

In fact, I didn't think our chances of survival were too good until we saw a little ship going by. It was sheer luck that a small tramp steamer called the *Baltrover* was going past on its way from Poland to Hull. Their engineer had gone up on deck for a breath of fresh air, and saw all the dinghies floating about, a lot of them empty. He radioed for assistance and a couple of Wessex choppers came out from Leconfield RAF base.

John Reeson, the Wessex winchman, said it was the first time they'd been out to a sinking drilling rig, and the worst rescue they had experienced.

The badly injured man, Cooper, went up first in the chopper.

Then the winchman went down into the water to try to get a line around this big guy called Sam Coull and, in doing so, some of the rubbish floating about in the sea ripped into his suit, so he was filling up with water. He was in a bit of a state. The crew got them both up, but Sam died on the chopper.

The next guy they picked out of the sea was one of the chefs, a young chap. Somebody said: 'He's copped it . . . ' He was dead. We couldn't believe it; we couldn't believe anyone had died. But a lot more had died because they'd been trapped under the drilling parts when the rig went down.

The lifeboat was floating along in the waves with one man in it, the radio operator, who had dived in the water and swam out to it; he was only nineteen, and a champion swimmer from Newcastle, but when he was plucked out of the water by the chopper he had frozen to death. I saw lots more bodies floating about. I didn't know which were dead, but I could see they were unconscious, and I thought: 'They ain't going to live much longer unless they get pulled out . . . ' I'd seen dead bodies before because I worked in bomb disposal in the war, so that didn't faze me at all, but these were people I had worked with for years. They were friends.

The little tramp ship lowered its net, and some of us scrambled up, which was the worst bloody job; I wish I hadn't attempted that. The crew said: 'Grab the net!' But the waves were knocking the dinghy into the ship, and we got knocked about. I only got halfway up, and I just froze on the net. No more energy, I couldn't do any more. They pulled us up and treated us with cognac and vodka, which certainly warmed us up. And then they ferried us into Hull, where the Salvation Army were waiting on the dock with hot tea and second-hand suits. I was knocked about a bit, mentally shattered too, seeing that lot happen, because I knew by then that so many had been killed.

Two of my drilling crew had died. Sam Coull was a Scot who had just come from Saudi Arabia to go on the North Sea, because it was like a home posting for him. He was the driller in charge of our group, but he was a bag of nerves. If you were on nights with him and something clanged or dropped, he'd go: 'What was that, Kevin? Did you hear that?' I wonder if he sensed something was going to happen. Bert Cooper died too. Bert was a nice bloke; cool, calm and collected, that was Bert. I knew him very well; we used to travel together.

They kept us in hospital overnight, and gave us a full MOT and then we were free to go.

They sent company transport to take us home. And when I got home there was a house full of practically everybody I knew in the world. Relatives had come from God knows where, and they all made a fuss. 'Here comes the hero ...' The doctor wouldn't let me go back to work, he said my leg wasn't right, and kept me off for six months. But I got fed up. I said to him: 'Look, it's time I went back.' I did go back to BP for a while, but they wanted me to go to Belfast where they were building a new rig, the *Sea Quest*. But I didn't fancy Belfast because of the troubles, so I said: 'I don't think I'll bother.' And I gave them notice, and went to work at the CEGB as a safety officer.

It was the old line afterwards, 'Lessons will be learned.' But lessons weren't learned, because the *Ocean Prince* went down not long after. Then there was the *Piper Alpha* – 157 men – and then there were more killed not long ago with the *Deepwater Horizon* in America, a BP rig again. To my knowledge, no one in our disaster ever claimed against the company, like they would today.

Fifteen out of thirty-nine died in our disaster. BP put it the other way round. In one of those books about the company they hand out to people, it says, 'Thirty-nine were killed and fifteen saved' – wrong way round. You'd think they'd get their facts right at least, wouldn't you? I knew all of those fifteen, and they were pretty good friends. I still miss them, and I went to lay a wreath not long ago because there'd been no ceremony at the time.

HUGO STACEY

I don't know why they didn't drop a bomb on us ...

I started training on Sea Kings towards the back end of 1981, just as the Falklands War was beginning to kick off. We were on HM *Argos*, doing a little bit of sea training, and there was suddenly this huge upsurge in squadron building, with more and more aircraft being sent out to the ships. We were then told we were going to join RFA *Fortgrange*, a Royal Fleet Auxiliary stores ship, which carried weapons, food, fuel and bombs, everything that a task force out in the Atlantic would need, and the plan was to continue our training on the way.

We flew to Plymouth, jumped on the ship and went up to one of the NATO arms depots in Scotland. For three days we had convoys of lorries bringing missiles, shells, depth charges and all manner of other ordnance, until the ship was absolutely full. Normally this stuff would all be stored down below, but we were carrying so much stuff it went everywhere, so you had missiles, food and aviation and ship fuel all stacked up together, and in order to get to your dinner you had to climb over piles of bombs.

We finally got underway, heading for Ascension Island. We crossed with HMS *Glasgow*, which was on her way home and wanting some fuel and food. *Glasgow* had been damaged by enemy fire – she'd had a bomb through the funnel – and we thought then: 'Ooh, yes, it's all kicking off down there ...' and it felt exciting. Anyway, we did a vertical replenishment at sea, what we call a 'razz', with *Glasgow*: you pick up the stores off the flight deck, run them across to the next ship, drop them down and go back and get some more. We got zoomed by an Argentinian Hercules during that razz, and the following day it came back and tried to bomb us again. It had already bombed one of the BP tankers the day before.

Someone said: 'It looks like it's passing on this side!' and everyone went around to the other side of the ship, although when you're on the largest pile of explosive in the Atlantic Ocean, going from one side of the ship to the other side is not going to make a huge amount of difference. If the ship had been hit, it would go bang, and it would go hugely. Actually, I don't know why they didn't drop a bomb on us, but, anyhow, they decided to give us a miss.

It got very warm towards Ascension Island, and then colder and rougher the further south we got, but we were comfortable, the ship had very good accommodation and the food was good. Where possible, we were given the opportunity to continue our training, but in this case there was a real ongoing, on-the-job learning, and we did our first bit of load-lifting by night in quite rough sea conditions.

We didn't go to the Falklands immediately, we went into an

operating box, called a COLA (carrier operating loitering area) and other ships needing food or fuel or arms came to us. On 11 July 1982, we were briefed to do a vertical replenishment with a relatively large ship called HMS *Leeds Castle*, an Island–class off-shore patrol vessel. For an hour and a half we were carrying food, beer, toilet rolls and all that sort of stuff across. Then we'd pick up the pallets and take them back so they could be reused.

We had just completed the last sortie, dropped the load on the flight deck of *Fortgrange*, and then gone into a hovering position alongside. I was flying from the left-hand seat and the other pilot, a chap called Frank Edwards, was in the right-hand seat. The two rear crew members were recovering a strop we'd been using for load-lifting, and the deck crew on *Fortgrange* were just wheeling away the last of the pallets. Flight deck height was fifty feet, and we were probably twenty feet above that, so we were about seventy feet, looking down and watching the deck crew. It was a position with good hover references on the ship, we had a reasonable amount of fuel and we felt very comfortable.

Then, without any warning, from being in control, with everything going our way, suddenly things began to go wrong. There was a distinctly loud noise from over our heads, then a lower note, then a crashing sound. On a Sea King you have two engines driving a rotor system; when you're quite light at the end of a sortie like we were, if one engine fails the rotor speed will have a tendency to decay, but the other engine will sense that decay, increase its output and provide enough power to maintain you in the hover. But what happened on this occasion was that when the number two engine failed, the number one engine didn't respond, and the aircraft descended immediately.

So, from being very cosy, looking down on the flight deck, we were now in the water looking up at the stern of the ship, which was about fifty foot above us, and disappearing into the distance at a rate of knots. The Sea King is built on a boat-type hull, so if it lands vertically on the water it can sit there for a while. We hit the surface in a bit of a nose-down attitude, which ripped the nose bay open, and cold water came scooting in up to our knees. We put the engine into a manual throttle to try and advance it and get airborne again, but it wasn't having it and just died.

The aircraft captain said: 'Right, following the standard operating procedure, everyone out of the aircraft ... ' And we all went: 'Frank, you must be having a laugh, it's freezing out there.' And he went: 'Oh yeah, I take your point.'

So we unstrapped and worked our way down to the back of the aircraft, gathering as much gear as we could – firearms, a camera and various other pieces of equipment. We had a ten-man dinghy and we all jumped into that. At that point we saw the number two engine was still burning at the back. In fact, there were some quite dramatic sheets of flame coming out of number two engine forward, indicating a massive breakdown within the engine, and we all paddled like mad to get away from it. Problem was, if you've got four people in a circular dinghy and they all start paddling, you just go round and round and round, but with the wind and our paddling efforts, we sort of bumped our way down the side of the aircraft until we were clear of it.

While all this had been going on, *Fortgrange* had turned around and was coming back, and *Leeds Castle* had launched a seaboat that came out to us; we jumped into their boat and they took us to the *Leeds Castle*. The sailors directed us down to the wardroom, and we were given a cigar and a choice of brandy or whisky, then the captain invited us up to the bridge to watch the attempt to rescue the aircraft.

Meanwhile, the crew of the *Fortgrange* seaboat was trying to add more flotation bags to the Sea King to keep it afloat. But it was a bit of a rough sea, and just as they came alongside they hit the side of the aircraft and burst one of the bags, at which point the aircraft started to turn over because it was now unbalanced, and the seaboat tipped over with it, dumping all eight rescuers into the water. I felt bad about that, because they were all immersed in the freezing water and we'd only got wet up to our knees.

Another Sea King from HMS *Invincible* came and started picking the men out of the water, and they were taken to *Fortgrange*, then the Sea King came back for us and took us to *Invincible* as well, where we waited for a flight to *Fortgrange*.

All the aircrew on 820 Squadron were desperately interested to hear what had happened, so we ended up in the bar, and as the tales went off we were bought more beer, so by the time we eventually got back into an aircraft – which was flown by Prince Andrew, funnily enough – we were pleasantly numb to the whole event.

When we walked into the hangar at *Fortgrange*, all the squadron maintainers immediately went: 'It wasn't our fault! We've been through all the books, and all the maintenance was done right . . .' There was real concern among them, which was quite heartening really. We had a word with the CO, then went off to get something to eat, watched a film in the wardroom, and then the flying programme for the next few days was announced: 'Right, you guys, you're off first thing.' And that was it. We just got on with life.

Compared to other Goldfish Club members we almost felt like cheats because we didn't actually get wet, but I wouldn't have wanted it to be any more exciting. It was quite exciting enough, thank you.

But even though I know the likely cause of the ditching was engine failure, there has always been a nagging doubt in my mind: was there something we missed? Was there an indication on the temperatures and pressures on the engine that we didn't see? The worst part is going over all that in your mind afterwards. But in point of fact, we got the aircraft from a catastrophic failure condition to a survivable impact, and everyone in the crew was fine, so we could be pleased about that. OK, they didn't save the aircraft in the end, but that was nothing to do with us.

RAY SCHILLINGER

Like it was Christmas ...

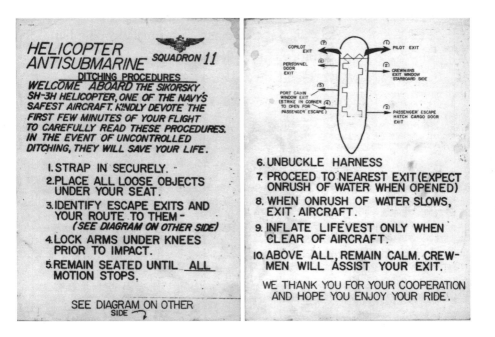

HELICOPTER
ANTISUBMARINE SQUADRON 11
DITCHING PROCEDURES
WELCOME ABOARD THE SIKORSKY
SH-3H HELICOPTER, ONE OF THE NAVY'S
SAFEST AIRCRAFT. KINDLY DEVOTE THE
FIRST FEW MINUTES OF YOUR FLIGHT
TO CAREFULLY READ THESE PROCEDURES.
IN THE EVENT OF UNCONTROLLED
DITCHING, THEY WILL SAVE YOUR LIFE.

1. STRAP IN SECURELY.
2. PLACE ALL LOOSE OBJECTS UNDER YOUR SEAT.
3. IDENTIFY ESCAPE EXITS AND YOUR ROUTE TO THEM –
   (SEE DIAGRAM ON OTHER SIDE)
4. LOCK ARMS UNDER KNEES PRIOR TO IMPACT.
5. REMAIN SEATED UNTIL ALL MOTION STOPS.

SEE DIAGRAM ON OTHER SIDE

COPILOT EXIT (7)   PILOT EXIT (1)
PERSONNEL DOOR EXIT (6)   CREWMANS EXIT WINDOW STARBOARD SIDE (2)
PORT CABIN WINDOW EXIT (5)
(STRIKE IN CORNER (4) TO OPEN FOR PASSENGER ESCAPE)   PASSENGER ESCAPE HATCH CARGO DOOR EXIT (3)

6. UNBUCKLE HARNESS
7. PROCEED TO NEAREST EXIT (EXPECT ONRUSH OF WATER WHEN OPENED)
8. WHEN ONRUSH OF WATER SLOWS, EXIT AIRCRAFT.
9. INFLATE LIFEVEST ONLY WHEN CLEAR OF AIRCRAFT.
10. ABOVE ALL, REMAIN CALM. CREWMEN WILL ASSIST YOUR EXIT.

WE THANK YOU FOR YOUR COOPERATION AND HOPE YOU ENJOY YOUR RIDE.

At the end of the day all boys want to fly. When I was a senior in high school I took flying lessons and got my private pilot's licence, and I actually left college with a commercial licence. The opportunity came to fly with the Navy, and I jumped at it.

I joined the military in Milton, Florida, going through Officer Candidate School, so regular *Officer and a Gentleman*-type stuff, and after graduating there I chose to go through a helicopter flight line, which was just the best fun, and December of 1984 I got designated a naval aviator and got my wings. From there, I was slotted to fly SH-3 Sea Kings.

January of 1987, I was in the Caribbean, on the *Teddy Roosevelt*, the USS *Theodore Roosevelt*, which is a nuclear carrier. A nuclear carrier is a floating city: you've got six thousand people on that ship, and it's literally like you're living in a small town, where you've got your hospitals, you've got your dentist, banks, an airport, a police department and fire department.

A routine NATOPS (Naval Air Training and Operating Procedures Standardization) flight check was scheduled, our yearly check ride. It was your typical Caribbean weather, sunny, warm, a very pleasant day . . .

It was a hot switch, so we were waiting on the flight deck; the plane landed, and the previous crew, who were our fellow squadron mates, just shut down the rotor and we went on board.

There was just time for a few words between the guys we were switching with:

'How is it out there?'

'Beautiful out there.'

'Anything maintenance or mechanical-wise?'

'No, nothing.'

We got ourselves strapped in and all set to go. We called up the tower, and the tower said, 'You can go.' And we went. There were four of us altogether. I was flying, but I had my plane commander to my left, and two sensor-operator crewmen in the back.

The check ride is a non-event, we've been through this a hundred times, a little bit of regular flying, a little bit of instrument flying, a couple of systems questions.

But, all of a sudden, my crewmen in the back began reporting that 'a lot of fluid' was coming from the ceiling. What do you mean, 'a lot' of fluid? we asked. Helicopters leak all the time. In fact, there's this standing joke in the helo community that if there's no leaking, that means the tank is empty. The guys weren't entirely sure what the problem was, but thought it was possible a line, or a major fitting had busted loose, or the actual transmission may have cracked . . .

And then all of a sudden things started going really bad. The high-speed shaft between the number two engine and the transmission fractured, and the engine began totally over-revving; you could hear bits and pieces of the driveshaft banging against the airframe and the transmission, it was incredibly noisy. Almost immediately after that we got an engine firelight, and then the annunciator panel, which is the big rack of warning lights, started lighting up like it was Christmas.

The ship wasn't all that far away, probably less than ten miles, but it was quite apparent we were not going to make it back to the ship; the NATOPS check ride was over, we were kind of flying for our lives now.

Paul Delian was the plane commander; it was now his call as to what to do . . .

Paul decided to do a controlled landing in the water, because helicopters without a transmission just don't fly. Paul was controlling the aircraft as best as he could. He tried to keep the control inputs to an absolute minimum, slowing us down, so that when we did go in the water it would be almost like a hover . . . But right at the last moment, the gearbox seized up; those last couple of feet before we impacted, there was no controllability, the aircraft just totally froze up, and there was nothing we could do, we were gone for the ride.

Oh God, the impact of hitting the water was absolutely terrifying, it was the loudest noise any of us had ever heard. We landed nose first, and the cockpit immediately filled up with water.

And then, boy, I hate to even say this, but it was every man for himself. Paul went out his window, and our crewmen at the back went out their respective windows. My end of the aircraft was underwater; I'd just had enough time to get a good solid breath of air in me before the water went over my head, and right after that the old-fashioned Navy training kicked in, which is all about trying to keep your cool. I got out of my window and swam up following the bubbles until I saw the sunlight.

All four of us swam towards each other until we were finally together. But I remember there was fuel in the water, which was deeply concerning because we carried smokes, which are flares you can drop, and some of those had started igniting upon impact. My first thoughts were: I've just survived an air crash, we need to get as far away as possible from the aircraft.

There was an F14 flying above, just keeping an eye on us, and after about ten minutes a helo came along and picked up two of us, and then another aircraft was immediately fired up, and picked up the other two.

When we got back to the ship, we were all taken down to Medical, who had the bunch of us lying down for a while just to make sure we were OK, while they checked out any cuts, bruises or shock, and stuff like that. The captain came by, as did the Fleet Admiral, and the priest, just to make sure we were OK, and then within an hour or two they let us go.

Our safety officer got to us almost immediately; he said, 'I want you to go to four separate rooms and write down everything that happened.' And we had to recollect everything for the accident investigation that was coming down the road. We all wrote pages and pages of affidavits of what we thought had happened. And then I was given a day off, although I was on the flight schedule the day after that.

I'm no longer in the Navy, but I actually have a photograph of the remains of my aircraft hanging up in my office, and when I've had a bad day, say the boss was beating up on me, all I have to do is to look at that picture, and think, Well, you've had at least one worst day, which kind of helps to keep things in perspective.

The Goldfish Club is an amazing collection of guys. When I heard about it, I put down my five pounds sterling a year, and joined. There are always cool stories from colleagues in the newsletters, although their stories tend to be way more exciting than mine, like this guy who had a Messerschmitt taking him downtown, or someone else who had been drifting in a stormy sea for several days after being shot down in the Second World War. Those guys are awesome.

JASON PHILLIPS

*One half was still Daddy, even if the other
half looked like the elephant man ...*

My father was a fighter pilot in the RAF who did his training during the war and went operational a couple of weeks
after VE Day. But in that short time he flew all the classics –
Tiger Moths, Harvards, Spitfires and Mustangs – and he passed

on his love of those planes, and I grew up fascinated with aircraft. The classic Spitfire was my dream plane, but anything that made a load of noise intrigued me, so, jet engines or the 'wocka, wocka' of helicopter blades giving it what for.

I wanted to be a pilot, but to qualify you must do a series of aptitude tests and I didn't have the hand-eye coordination. To improve it, I spent a year playing squash, and the very primitive computer games they had in those days, and then one day I suddenly thought, My God, why am I putting myself through this? So observer was the route for me, and I wouldn't change it now: as an observer, you are the navigator, the tactician and the warrior, whereas the pilots are just the taxi drivers.

The Sea King Mk VI was the aircraft I trained on, and I flew that for ten years, as near as dammit.

In 1988 I was on 820 Squadron, having done two front-line tours; on 3 September we were flying to Holland on a liaison visit, prior to an exercise later in the year.

You always listen to the distress channels en route, so if someone has an emergency they can yell out on there and everyone will hear them. As we flew across the Channel, we could hear an emergency going on; a Jaguar had ditched in the Wash, and, indeed, the aircraft commander called up and asked if we could render assistance, but someone else took the call and an RAF search and rescue helo was on its way.

We were greeted by the Dutch, and went on board their ship to discuss our future liaison, and went ashore that evening, had something to eat and some guys got on the train and went into Amsterdam on a run ashore, as we call it in the Navy, for the usual delights of that place. I didn't go, because before we'd really had the chance to cut loose and properly enjoy ourselves myself and the senior pilot got a phone call from the squadron air engineer for us to be on standby to locate the wreck of the Jaguar that had ditched, which just made us think, OK, we've got to be alert tomorrow.

Sure enough, the next morning the tasking came through to locate the Jaguar, or at least where the beacon was: all military aircraft have a beacon on them and when that goes into salt water it emits a tone. Our orders were to go to RAF Coltishall, and stage out of there.

When we got to Coltishall, the BBC TV programme *Top Gear* was there, racing some performance car along the runway against a Jaguar fighter jet. Also that night there was going to be a party in the officers' mess to mark Battle of Britain Day, and at the end of the night everyone would go out to a balcony where a Jaguar would do some screamy flypast. I was thinking, we'll be back by then, and we could follow the Jaguar at about sixty knots in our Sea King, with a Navy ensign out on the winch wire, as ever giving the RAF one up from the Navy, and then get stuck into the cocktail party.

Before take-off, we briefed the position they had for the wreckage. The Sea King has active dipping sonar so we planned to position ourselves at certain distance around that point, put the sonar in, listen, and if we went to different locations around it, we could triangulate where the beacon was.

The senior pilot on this flight was Lieutenant Commander Rory McNeile, who was originally a Lynx helicopter man; the second pilot was Lieutenant Charlie Parrock, a very dear friend of mine, and the aircrewman was Warrant Officer Aircrewman Sox Glover, the most senior aircrewman we had.

Although it was a beautiful warm evening, Rory made us wear goon bags, which are big, thick immersion suits, with rubber seals around the neck and wrists, designed to keep you dry and warm should you end up in the water. Fifteen degrees centigrade water temperature is normally the cut-off as to whether we wear them or not, but the water temperature was seventeen degrees and I remember thinking, I can't believe Rory is making us wear goon bags in this warm weather. But I didn't say anything, because, at the end of the day, he was the aircraft commander and the authoriser, so it was his decision.

We took off at roughly five o'clock. It was a beautiful Friday afternoon, clear blue sky, just a perfect day to be doing stuff that was a bit out of the ordinary, with a great bunch of guys. Going on an adventure is what it felt like.

We went out to where the lat-long was, about thirty-odd miles away from Coltishall, and went down into the dips. The aircraft went into a hover at forty feet, and we put the sonar body in the water. We listened and could detect the beacon straight away on the observer's radar screen. We drew a line straight down that bearing, then we jumped – which is when the aircraft comes up from forty feet, goes to two hundred feet, then flies along – to the next position. 'Stand by to mark. Dip. Mark now.' So we've now got two bearings, so there's a cross cut. Finally, we went for the third jump, just to get the classic midshipman's fix, as we would call it in the Navy, where all three of the lines cross. We went down into the dip for the third time, put the sonar body in the water and we were all thinking, We'll be at that cocktail party before long, when, all of a sudden, a big load of flame suddenly appeared in the back of the aircraft, directly in front of where Sox and I were sitting.

I remember thinking at first, Bloody hell, that's quite impressive, how have the front seat managed to do that?, because there's always a lot of banter going on between front and back, before thinking, Don't be an idiot, this is not some trick they have organised for us . . .

Suddenly, the aircrewman, Sox, was up out of his seat, covered in flames, and he was yelling and screaming. Oh, bloody hell, I thought, this is a bit terminal. I got out of my seat too, because now the whole area in front of me was on fire. The guys up front couldn't see anything in the back, but they could hear us. Charlie Parrock said afterwards he just thought it was the wimpy guys down the back making some unnecessary fuss about something or other.

Anyway, my first thought was, I need to try to put the flames out, but there was no fire extinguisher to hand; the nearest one was at the back of the aircraft. So I decided to try to put the flames out with my hands. I would normally have been wearing single-leather gloves, but for whatever reason I was wearing winching gloves, which have got a second layer of protective cloth. Not only did I not put out the flames, but I successfully set fire to both my hands. Suddenly, I began thinking of Christopher Plummer in the film *Battle of Britain*, which was my father's favourite film. There's a bit when he's in his Hurricane, and he's on fire, and I thought, I'm now in exactly the same situation as dear old Christopher.

The pilots have a mirror in the front of the aircraft – which we

213

always say is for them to see how good they're looking – but this time they looked in the mirror and saw a fireball coming forward from the cabin, and they made the decision to ditch, although I didn't hear the order, 'Prepare for ditching', because at some point I had come out of my leads. So I wasn't braced for ditching, and I remember thinking, I'm in a real bad place here, because I'm not strapped in.

But we hit the water upright and, bearing in mind we were at forty feet, we didn't have that far to go, so the landing was not too bad. However, for whatever reason, in the impact of hitting the water the cargo door came open maybe three or four inches and water started to pour in. I remember thinking that would make a really nice water feature for a garden ...

The aircraft was now filling up with water, and I realised it was time to take that final breath and get ready to exit. So I took a deep breath, and, opening my eyes underwater, I could see the natural light coming in through the cargo-door window, and I focused on that window, just like some *Star Wars*-type tractor beam.

I saw Sox swim through. Right, that's the way for me to go. But I got stuck going through the window: my seat pack, which was made of hard, very toughened plastic, had got snagged. As the seconds ticked away, I reached a period of calm, it was quite surreal, actually ... *I could stay here or I could get out* ... But I thought of my children and I reached behind me, pushed my seat pack down and popped out through the window, kicked myself off the side of aircraft and came to the surface. I saw Sox and Rory McNeile, and we all began yelling to each other, and then Charlie appeared from the front of the aircraft, because he had gone out through a different window,

214

and that feeling of seeing all their three heads on the surface, really, it was the most awesome feeling, better than sex. My God, we're all alive!

I was conscious that I had seen Sox covered in flames, shouting and screaming, and he was an old bloke, he must have been in his forties – the age I am now – and I thought he might be really badly hurt. I went over and grabbed hold of him, and the pair of us swam over to where the pilots were and got in their dinghy. When I asked Sox why he had been screaming, it turned out that years ago someone told him if ever he was in an accident in a helicopter the best course of action was to get yourself on the floor and scream your head off, and so that's what he was doing. I never did understand the reasoning behind that.

Anyway, as we all sat there, awaiting rescue, people started asking me with real concern, 'Are you all right, Jas? Are you OK?' I had been completely unaware that half of my face had been burned. But, as time went on it started to hurt, almost as much as my hands, which I was trailing in the water.

A fishing boat came along and offered to take us on board, but there was a six-foot freeboard to climb up on the side, so I said to the lads, 'In my condition, I'm not going to be able to climb up there.' So they said, 'No, we're all right, thank you very much.'

There's plenty of gas rigs off the Norfolk coast, and a red Bond helicopter going out to the rigs then turned up and we all got ready for him to come and pick us up, but it turned out he didn't have a winch, so he just flew around and we waved to indicate we were OK.

★

Fortunately, when we fly we have a system where we have to make op normal calls every twenty minutes. Well, we'd just made a call at about six o'clock, and ditched very soon after, and a very alert person in the tower at Coltishall noticed that our radar return had disappeared and had asked aircraft to assist. A couple of F15s elected to come and have a look, and they radioed in that they could see life rafts in the water. So then a fully spammed-up search and rescue operation came into play. We'd been in the water fifty minutes when an RAF helicopter turned up, and we were winched aboard, pretty grateful for the goon bags because the water felt distinctly chilly.

Once we were in the aircraft, I really started to hurt. My face was stinging, and my hands were killing me, although fortunately they had some eyewash bottles in the aircraft and were squeezing drops into my gloves to keep my hands irrigated. Their aircrewman kindly offered to cut my gloves off using a J-knife, which has a really sharp blade that is designed to cut through parachute lines, but I thought, I don't really want to see whatever's underneath this leather, so I declined his offer. I'd seen my hands on fire, and I had this vision that when the gloves were taken off there was just going to be skeleton.

The RAF lads took us to a field near Norwich Hospital, where two ambulances were waiting for us. Rory and Sox went in an ambulance where they had a female paramedic, and Charlie and I ended up in the ambulance that had a male paramedic, and I remember him saying, 'Why have they got the female? Why haven't we got the female?' But by this stage I was really starting to worry about what mess I might have at the end of my arms, so I said, 'Charlie, do shut up, I'm really worried about what's going on here . . .'

Anyway, the ambulance took us to Norwich Hospital, where I was given morphine, and then someone cut my gloves off, and my wedding ring, and I was delighted to see I still had flesh. Also, I managed to phone home and speak to my wife, and tell her what had happened. Naturally she was worried about me, but she was all right; she's a one in a million. And she's very tolerant of my life in the Navy.

Our maintainers from Coltishall turned up at the hospital with a bag of clothes for us, and I got changed as best I could without use of my hands, and we headed back to Coltishall, where I was dropped off in the sickbay, and the others went to the Battle of Britain Day cocktail party, which was still going on. Everyone was asking them, 'Why are you guys in flying overalls? 'Oh, we've just ditched . . . ' they nonchalantly replied and they became instant celebrities, and were fed brandy all night.

Meanwhile, I finally looked at myself in a mirror and saw what a mess I was in. The left half of my face was completely burned, there were blisters and scabs all over me; several people who came to visit couldn't actually look at me. Also, I kept getting these wet feelings on my face, which were blisters bursting, which was very uncomfortable, and they had put my hands in clear plastic bags, and various bits and pieces were constantly dropping into them . . . it was all quite unpleasant.

We returned to RNAS Culdrose, our home base. They sent a Jetstream, which is one of the training aircraft, to come and pick us up. And when they flashed up the aircraft, loads of smoke from the air conditioning started to come up from under the seats and I remember sitting there, thinking, My God, what's happening, is this aircraft on fire too? But we flew back to Culdrose without incident, and taxied right up to the front door. My wife and kids were upstairs in a crew room, so I was allowed to go and see them right away. They were a bit horrified at first, particularly my youngest, who at the time was very small, but they could see that one half was still Daddy, even if the other half looked like the elephant man.

Every day for the next few weeks I went to sickbay, where they would treat my burns, recoat them and put new plastic bags on my hands. Eventually, they decided to cut off all the blisters with a scalpel, and then I did make sure that when I was around the kids I had a pillowcase I could put my hands into, because once they took the blisters off I had open sores dripping blood, and fluid, and all sorts everywhere, which wasn't very nice to look at and was incredibly painful. The blisters would get so big. My fingertips were particularly badly blistered, and on one occasion I thought, this hurts so much, I've got to relieve it, and I stabbed a pin into a blister and when I took the pin out the fluid hit me in the eye.

I was off flying until my hands were well enough to be able to put on gloves, which I needed to do, because with the Sea King, which is perennially dripping oil, I'd end up getting some hideous infection without them.

Anyway, that's my ditching story, and other than swapping stories at the annual Goldfish dinners I don't often think about it. Funnily enough, though, just a few days ago I woke up in the middle of the night; we have a small portable television in our bedroom and when I turned it on they were showing *Battle of Britain*. It was exactly the moment when Christopher

Plummer was alight in his aircraft, not five seconds before, or five seconds after, and although I've seen that film twenty-five or thirty times I had to watch it again just to make sure he got out.

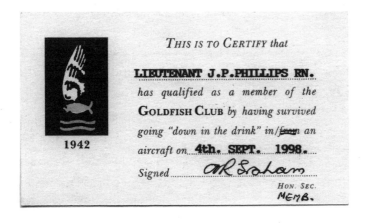

THIS IS TO CERTIFY that

LIEUTENANT J.P.PHILLIPS RN.

has qualified as a member of the GOLDFISH CLUB by having survived going "down in the drink" in/~~from~~ an aircraft on 4th. SEPT. 1998.

Signed ....

HON. SEC.
MEMB.

1942

MIKE DANE

It's very quiet when the engine stops . . .

Left to right: Eric Leyden, David Crawford, Mike Dane, John Reynell

The Korean War was on and the Royal Air Force was recruiting like mad, and they came round to my grammar school in Shrewsbury and interviewed us. I was selected, but then had to wait until I was old enough to join, but I joined

221

in March 1953, about three weeks after my eighteenth birth-day.

Initially I was trained as a wireless operator and air gunner, and the first squadron I was on flew Shackletons, but then I went to search and rescue helicopters. We used Whirlwinds. The Whirlwind was a single-engine helicopter, and in those early days it had a radial engine that was very underpowered; later on they put jet engines in them and solved the power problem.

There were three crew; I was the winchman, the one who goes down on the cable to rescue the person in trouble; the winch operator was Flight Lieutenant David Crawford, and Eric Leyden was the pilot.

We were stationed at Manston in Kent. We'd sit in the crew room, and when the scramble bell went off we would rush out to the helicopter, and you never knew what you were going to find. You could do land or cliff rescues, mountain rescues, or someone might be in the sea, clinging on to a boat, or they might even be in the boat, but in distress.

Practically my first rescue we were called out to a canoeing expedition that had gone wrong: a bunch of Boy Scouts were doing some sort of Outward Bound-type thing, and the sea was far too rough, and they had got into terrible trouble. I picked up eight or nine boys one after the other from those canoes.

We were called out one morning, and there was a ship on fire: the crew had abandoned it with the engine running and it was sailing along on its own. I went down to it, and, as the only person on it, technically I took possession of the ship on behalf of the Royal Air Force. In fact, I got a letter from the Crown Solicitor awarding me seventy pounds' salvage money, which in those days was not an unreasonable amount of money.

Another time we were called to the Isle of Sheppey, where a yacht had capsized, and this woman was in the sea, with her arms stretched out, her eyes wide open and she wasn't blinking. She'd been in the water a long time, at least an hour, and it was winter, early January; in fact, she was so frozen solid that I couldn't bend her arms to put the strop on her. Eventually I succeeded, although as we went up in the cradle I remember looking at the winch operator and I gave him a thumbs down, because I was convinced this woman was dead. Anyway, we got her into the cabin, put her into a blanket, and, lo and behold, she blinked. We got her to hospital, and she was OK from there, fully recovered. Amazing! I remember the RAF medical people were very interested in this woman, and followed up her case to try to find out how she'd managed to survive for so long in a sea temperature that should have killed her.

In October '61, we were doing a demonstration for the Royal National Lifeboat Institution, in particular the Ramsgate Lifeboat, who were having a flag day to collect money. Our search and rescue unit had only been going for three months, and this was our first exercise with the lifeboats. We were doing a winching exercise just off the beach at Ramsgate, where I would go down to the lifeboat, pick up a 'survivor', who was one of the squadron pilots, in this case an RAF guy called Reynell, take him up to the helicopter and put him back down again. It was just for demonstration purposes, but it was the sort of thing we did for real and a lot of people had assembled on the shore to watch.

When the demonstration was over, the lifeboat shot off – I think they went to look at their lobster pots several miles away – and we went further out to sea, and started wet-winching training.

After that was finished, we were in the harbour, about fifty feet above the sea, stationary. I was sitting in the doorway with my feet outside the aircraft – in those days the waterproofing in the helicopters was very basic, and we used to hang outside as long as we could to drain off the seawater to try and avoid getting saltwater in the aircraft, which was made of aluminium, and would just corrode.

As the helicopter started to move away and climb, Dave Crawford clambered up into the left-hand seat next to the pilot – and accidentally turned the fuel cock off, and the engine stopped right away, because it had no petrol. I can tell you it's very quiet when the engine stops, unbelievably silent.

A helicopter has to take account of height–velocity ratio, or 'dead man's curve' as it's called by some pilots. A helicopter can still be controlled if the engine stops, but you need one of two things: you either need plenty of height, at least four hundred feet, because then, as it falls through the air, the wind through the rotors will keep them turning, which means that the pilot can still fly it; or, you need plenty of forward speed, something like a hundred miles an hour. It's got to be one or the other.

The problem was we had no height and no speed, so we were always going to do what we did, which was fall straight into the sea. We were in the sea within seconds. I was still sitting in the open door, and as we hit the sea the water washed me into the cabin, and I could see nothing but millions and millions of little bubbles. Very fortunately, there was an air pocket in the back of the cabin into which we were thrown.

The blades hit the sea, and, because they were high, as they came around they chopped the tail off the helicopter and one of the rotor blades was embedded even further down the body in the side of it, and the front end was smashed.

Well, I thought I was going to die, because when we hit the water the helicopter then rolled over – helicopters invariably turn upside down because all the weight is in the roof. But there is a little plastic window in the back, which is an escape window really. I just punched it out – it was designed for that – and I can vividly remember the relief that came over me as my body slid through the gap. Reynell came next, and we both had immersion suits on, which were buoyant, so naturally we floated to the surface. We found the winch operator already in the sea; he had got out through the top left-hand window. I was very glad to see him.

The aircraft then sank in about thirty seconds, with the pilot in it, and he went a long way down too, thirty or forty feet, but fortunately he was a sub-aqua person and kept his wits about him, and managed to free himself. He'd already blown up his life jacket, and he came out of the water like a cork from a champagne bottle, almost up to his knees – we actually saw him shoot up.

So there we all were, and as we floated in the water we asked each other if we were OK, and we were all OK, and I remember the four of us laughing our heads off in the water, waiting for the lifeboat to come.

The lifeboat charged across and picked us up, and we were

taken to sick quarters to see if we'd had any physical damage – in those days there was no such thing as counselling, or any of that rubbish – and we had no ill effects whatsoever from our escapade, and the next day we were sent up in the air again.

Was it a near-death experience? Well, it could have been, but as it turned out it wasn't, so I don't think it affected any of us really.

One little footnote of interest. There were several hundred people watching this demonstration, and we were told afterwards that almost everyone ran to find the nearest telephone after we'd ditched – this was long before mobile phones, of course – and dialled 999, saying, 'a helicopter's just crashed in the sea ...' In those days every reasonable-sized town had its own exchange, and each exchange had only so many emergency lines, and it was arranged that if all the lines were engaged at once, they'd be automatically transferred to the next exchange, and somebody told us afterwards that we'd blocked every 999 line all over the county of Kent.

DEREK FIDDAMAN

'In God's name, what have we done...?'

I joined the Navy as an ordinary simple sailor, a seaman. The Cod War was on, and I was sent up to HMS *Russell*, an anti-submarine frigate, which was operating out of Rosyth, going around Iceland chasing fishery boats around the place. The British were fully entitled to fish up there, but the Icelanders didn't like it because they called it their water, and they were nasty about it; they'd go and crash into our fishing boats, and made themselves very unpopular. So we were there to try and stop all that, but, of course, they were never around when we were, although it was quite good fun chasing them.

At that time they were asking for volunteers for aircrew, and after you'd had so many years' sea time you could apply to become helicopter aircrew. Basically, you'd jump into an aircraft, the pilot would throw it around The Lizard, and if you didn't get airsick you were suitable.

I loved it from the word go. The *Dragonfly* was where we learned how to use the winch and do rescue work; it was a lovely aircraft, very simple, a bubble on three wheels, with a rotor and a tail fan. And then it was on to the big choppers. The Wessex were very much in their infancy back then, and not all that safe; we used to lose one about every ten days or so.

At that time we were essentially an anti-submarine helicopter squadron, flying off HMS *Hermes*. My specialist qualification was anti-submarine warfare: we'd go and do a screen, where we'd be inside the aircraft, listening for enemy subs. In those days it was very basic; you just dropped your sonar boom down below the surface and it would echo back whatever it hit, whether it be a whale, a dolphin, another ship, a submarine, a wreck or a tide rip, and you'd have to tell the difference with your ears. If you did find a sub, you'd just say to yourself, 'Got you, you bastard!' although, potentially, it was a dangerous thing to do because a submarine could come straight below the dome, and chuck a missile up your chuff. Believe it or not, one of the noisiest things underwater is a shrimp; it rubs its back legs together like a cricket, and the amplified noise is deafening. Whales are marvellous, I could listen to whales for hours: I'd get quite emotional listening to them, it's just a lovely sound, *whooooo* . . . We'd be up in the Arctic, and you'd hear a whale call, and then the same tone would come from another whale hundreds of miles away, and they'd talk to each other. Amazing.

On 15 January 1963 we were flying in a Wessex, operating off HMS *Hermes*, not far off the Philippines in the South China Sea. It was a happy time on the *Hermes*; we had a very, very good crowd, all nice blokes – although I have not met one bad air-crewman in all my time.

We were a good ten miles away from the ship when the aircraft started juddering, just doing things it shouldn't do, and I could feel my sphincter going sixpences and half-crowns. I'd still got the sonar dome hanging down twenty feet, so I immediately put the G-lock on, and asked Frank Hillyer, the first pilot, a dead laconic Queenslander, what was going on. He said, 'I don't know, but I can't hold this flaming thing ...'

'Well, let me get the gear up,' I said, and I was trying to get the dome back in, because, if you're going to go in the water, you don't want electrics around you. But, halfway through that, the aircraft started juddering again, even more strongly; there was definitely something wrong with the aircraft. 'OK,' Frank said, 'we're going back. Pan. Pan. Pan. 643 returning to Mother ...' But halfway through the turn, Frank said, 'Oh shit! I can't hold this flaming thing ... Mayday, Mayday, flaming Mayday, 643 ditching.' Oh God, my fingers were flying all over the place, trying to switch everything off, which was difficult, bearing in mind this was at night-time.

Your blades will break if they are going round when they hit the water, and that obviously throws the aircraft around a bit, and the aircraft will eventually flip over on its back because of the rotor gear. And that's exactly what happened. I found myself at the back of the aircraft all on my own, but then my finger touched fresh air – how, I don't know – so I then knew exactly which way was up. I did a very good imitation of Jesus Christ: I didn't just walk on the water, I ran on it. I was that scared, I make no bones about it.

I was floating around for a couple of minutes before I remembered I'd got a Mae West, and I pulled the toggle and it inflated around me, and everything sprung into action. I then heard this *sssssh* behind me, which was another dinghy inflating, and I said, 'What are you doing Frank?' 'Getting into my flaming dinghy ... bloody big fish around here, mate. I'm talking sharks!' So I let my dinghy inflate under me also.

The aircraft had disappeared by this time; she'd gone under. The other two crew, Mike Burse, the second pilot, and George Brown, the observer, had got out the starboard side of the aircraft, and started swimming towards us, so in the end we tied the four dinghies together, which was the sensible thing to do.

Having made sure we were all OK, we thought we'd better get in touch with our ship, so we popped out our SARBEs, search and rescue beacon equipment, which are carried on the Mae West. I'm laying back in the dinghy going ... 'Mother, Mother, Mother, this is yellow jacket, yellow jacket ...' and all of a sudden a shout came back: 'Transmit for bearing.' OK. Actually, *Hermes* didn't come for us because she was firing off fixed-wing aircraft at the time, but they sent the escort destroyer for us and she came hurtling through the sea. And when they got near us they just sort of spun round, dropped the seaboat, scooped us up and took us back to *Hermes*. Some medical officer came up to us, and asked, 'You all right?' and we said, 'Fine, no problem.' 'OK, report for a medical in the morning.'

I eventually got my head down and went to sleep, and we were flying the following morning, doing what they called general flying practice.

I was only in the water for a relatively short time; some of these wartime fellows were in the drink for days and days: they're the heroes, especially when you think how basic their safety equipment was. OK, because of the surface area of a big bomber it would float for a longer period than a helicopter – you've got maybe ninety seconds to get out of a helicopter. But, of course, they'd also been shot at, and were probably wounded or bleeding.

That wasn't my only mishap at sea. Six years earlier, in 1957, I was on a destroyer, HMS *Cossack*, out in the Far East, and we were sent to Christmas Island in the Pacific for the H-bomb tests. The British Nuclear Tests were a whole series of test runs, 1952 through to 1963. Nobody ever told us about the dangers of nuclear radiation, and that's what all these scars are from on my face and back: skin cancer. Believe it or not, there are two hundred scars on my face and back – skin grafts have been the story of my life since 1975.

I only saw the one explosion, and it was the most frightening sight I've ever seen in my life. It was 8 November 1957; it was called Operation Grapple X, and it was a test explosion of one of the first thermonuclear hydrogen bombs.

We had initially been sent to chase off a tramp steamer, SS *Effie* was her name, which was sailing between the islands delivering a bit of this and collecting a bit of that. We signalled and signalled, but they were all asleep down below, so we had to go right down and tell her she was in a dangerous area, that a big bomb was going to go off very shortly and they were heading toward it. We eventually got them cleared, and then we had to go to Fanning Island to pick up some scientists and take them down to Port London on Christmas Island.

As we were steaming north, we heard the bomb was about to go off the starboard bow about twenty, twenty-five miles away. The captain said, 'OK everybody, sit down on the opposite side of the ship,' so we all went to the port side of the ship and sat down and covered our eyes with our hands.

The captain then said, 'I'll count down until the explosion,' so he went from ten to zero, and then there was this almighty BANG, and I remember someone next to me said, 'In God's name, what have we done . . .?'

We all stood up and turned around, and there was this fireball, and it looked like it was being sucked up into the heavens; it just rose up higher and higher into the air, and you then had an enormous mushroom cloud, with the reds and the blacks rolling around, and it got bigger and bigger, and it looked as if the ocean was on fire: oh, it was a terrifying sight. And then we got the shock wave, and even from that that distance it was a hell of a force, the ship vibrated quite badly, and we all were shaken too, of course. So frightening.

In 1980 all the records were released which finally proved that the troops who were around those explosions were used as guinea pigs. But, to this day, the government has denied it, and has spent millions trying to prove that none of us were exposed, even though every other country in the world, including China and Russia, have paid all the veterans compensation.

The upshot of it is that out of the twenty thousand-odd men who were on Christmas Island over that period there are probably only 1500 or 1600 left alive, plus there's a lot of widows out there with very deformed children. I've lost so many friends and colleagues, and seen so many women suffering with deformed children that I've lost count. But the government still denies it, the MOD denies it all the time.

However, please God, hopefully the judges in the Supreme Court will listen to the science now, because science has now proved that, yes, we were exposed. You have to prove that the physical complaints we've got are attributable to nuclear radiation received from the nuclear tests in the South Pacific and Australia. We can't prove it. It's inhuman.

I'm very bitter and very angry. I'm angry with the politicians of the past and the present for not having the guts to stand up to civil servants and the MOD, and say, 'You will compensate these men.'

BILL STONEMAN

'Old Stoney's got away with it again ...'

I was only fifteen when the Second World War started, but I remember the fear and worry of it all in my home very well, because a lot of my family had suffered in the First World War. My father had lost a younger brother, Christopher, who died in

Mesopotamia; he died of thirst in the trenches, and when they found his body his tongue had swollen up in his face. My father had gone to America when he was seventeen, like a lot of chaps who wanted to get on in the world. But he came straight home when war was declared, and as soon as he landed in Liverpool he walked into a recruitment centre and joined the Lancashire Fusiliers, and wore a hat with a plume, even though he was a Cornishman born and bred.

He was wounded by shrapnel and sent back home with all these shell fragments in his back. They were just the size of a fingernail, only little slivers, and they'd work their way out of his body and you could pull them out, and within a day or two the scar had gone. I must have taken out dozens of pieces in my lifetime.

I was young at the beginning of the war, and all I wanted to know was 'When can I do my bit?' I wanted to be a pilot. I went for RAF aptitude testing at eighteen, and passed as a PNB – pilot, navigator or bomb aimer. But I was told it would be six to eight months before I would be called up to fly, which seemed a lifetime, and the only way to join straight away was to become a rear gunner. So that's what I did, with the idea of remustering to a pilot later on. But once I started flying missions over occupied territory I knew I could never be anything else. Most attacks from German night fighters – the Focke-Wulfs and the Messerschmitts in particular – came from behind, and as the rear gunner you're the one person the whole crew relies on at the moment of attack.

After air gunnery training, I was sent to RAF Gamston in Nottinghamshire. There were gunners of every nationality there, lots of Americans, Canadians and Australians, but the British were the most sought-after because our training was considered a little bit special. I remember walking towards the hangar one morning and two Canadians, a pilot called Sid Godfrey and a navigator, Don Lennie, came roaring out and grabbed me. They said: 'You can fly with us,' so we crewed up with them and flew Wellingtons together.

At the beginning of 1943, we were sent to RAF Dishforth in North Yorkshire where we joined the 1664 Heavy Conversion Unit to retrain on Halifaxes. Don Lennie had been a bank clerk before the war, but he turned out to be a simply outstanding navigator. There weren't the navigation aids we have today, it was all down to dead reckoning and mathematical calculation, taking in air speed and crosswinds, but Don was better than a computer. On only one occasion did he get it a bit wrong: we went on a training mission over the North Sea and, coming back during a heavy snowstorm, we came in so low over the coast that we missed York Minster by about a hundred feet. I remember Sid saying: 'Christ, that's the nearest I've been to church in years.' We had a special rapport, Sid and I. But we were all getting well above average marks, and we just gelled as a crew, so much so that at the end of the course the commanding officer sent for us and told us we were going to stay in Bomber Command, but we weren't going to drop bombs on target cities, we were to join a special duty squadron, dropping live agents and supplies to freedom fighters in the occupied territories.

In February we were posted to RAF Tempsford to join 138 Special Duties Squadron, which was tasked with dropping agents and equipment for the Special Operations Executive (SOE). The

SOE's mission was to facilitate espionage, sabotage and reconnaissance behind enemy lines. We had to fly low-level, because
we dropped agents from about eight hundred feet and supplies
from six hundred feet. We flew to all the occupied countries,
Poland, Czechoslovakia, Holland, Norway, Denmark, France,
dropping agents into fields more or less by torchlight. Those
blokes were incredibly brave, and the navigators in the planes had
to be first class in order to drop them dead on target, because if
those blokes were caught they weren't taken prisoner, they were
shot.

You never knew where danger was coming from. I remember,
flying over France, we started our approach to make the drop and
the pilot was getting us down to five or six hundred feet, but
there were a couple of German armoured cars down below,
streaking along a straight road at sixty or seventy miles per hour,
hitting us hard with gunfire, which felt as though Fred Astaire
was dancing on the aircraft.

Sid Godfrey, my pilot, was shot down on his first trip without
me and spent the rest of the war in a POW camp, so suddenly I
was without a crew. The commanding officer asked if I'd stay on
as spare gunner, which meant I'd only fly when another rear
gunner was sick, or had been killed. In ten months I flew thirty-
two missions with thirteen different crews, which I understand
is a record. When you've been lucky and survived some near
misses, you get a good name. People would say, 'Old Stoney's got
away with it again . . .' when I got back safely once more, and I
was considered a bit of a good-luck mascot, someone people
wanted to have along on their flights.

In July 1944 we set off on a trip to drop supplies and agents in the South of France. We flew to Blida airfield in North Africa, where we had one night's rest in a tent while the aircraft was refuelled and loaded with supplies and ammunition. It was extremely hot and dusty and uncomfortable, and we couldn't wait to leave. We took off the following evening, and we were over the Mediterranean, about sixty miles from Blida, when we were hit by a Luftwaffe Junkers 88. They were awesome machines: its pilot just sat in his aircraft underneath us, locked on to us with his radar and then let loose this cannon shot, which must have been of quite a big calibre because there was one hell of a bang.

I didn't see any fire, but I could smell burning fuel, and the aircraft just fell from the sky like a sycamore seed. The pilot was a Canadian flight lieutenant called Hi Walker, who had already been awarded a Distinguished Flying Cross. He was at his physical limit trying to get control of this falling aircraft, because I could hear him breathing very hard over the intercom. And through brilliant airmanship, at the very last moment he managed to steady the plane and pancake on to the sea.

The nose had obviously gone, because as soon as the aircraft hit the sea it filled with water, and we were up to our waists. Not only did the Halifax have fuel tanks in the wings, it had more in the fuselage, and I think those overload tanks must have burst too, because the stink of fuel and seawater was awful, really distressing, and our eyes were streaming.

There was an escape hatch above the spar, just big enough for a man to get through; I gave the handle half a turn, chucked it away and climbed out. The dinghy should have come out automatically when it touched water, but no bloody dinghy appeared.

But that wasn't the biggest worry at that moment: the chaps were all in a terrible way and calling out, and I managed to get each of them out through the hatch – with them scrambling and me pulling – bar the navigator. I couldn't find the navigator.

My next thought was: We really need this bloody dinghy, because we're sinking . . . so I had to go back into the aircraft with the bomb aimer holding my harness. It was dark, but with the reflection of the moon on the water I could just see enough to find the handle, which had a D for Dinghy on it. I turned it, and heard the hissing, so I knew it was inflating, and, sure enough, the bit of the wing which should release fell away and out it popped. I got into the water with the dinghy and managed to paddle it back and get the blokes into it.

The flight engineer was unconscious, the pilot had very badly damaged hands – he must have smashed them as we hit, because they were bleeding quite profusely – and the rest were in a bad state too, plus we were all wet through and stinking of aviation fuel. In the dark, we watched the Halifax start to sink. The front went first until just the tail fins of the plane were sticking up. And then we heard a shout for help come from inside the aircraft. It was the navigator, Tony Farr, who must have just gained consciousness. I heard him call out twice. 'Help.' 'Help.' But it was too late, the aircraft was just gobbled up by the water, and she sank with him inside. I felt awful, really, really awful. Although I'd only flown with him a couple of times, I knew he was married, the only married man in the crew, and I understand he had a little girl too.

We were only in the water for fifty minutes when we were spotted by an Italian hospital ship, the *Principesse Giovanna*, which just happened to be in the Med taking wounded Berbers home to North Africa. The Berbers were awesome warriors, and were used by the French rather like we used our Gurkhas. We were taken into sick quarters on board, and I was put into a cot, with 'shock and exhaustion' written on a label at the end of my cot.

Those Berbers were interesting fellows; whenever these Berbers captured or killed a prisoner, they'd take an ear off as a trophy. Andy Spooner, our flight engineer, woke up after being unconscious for twenty-four hours, and there were all these grinning black men in their dyed white beards right to the ground, clustered around his bed, showing him their little leather bags full of ears. He thought he'd died and gone to hell.

We were dropped off at Oran in Algeria, and sent straight to the American hospital there, where we spent about ten days recovering. I didn't need those ten days in hospital, not really. I was all right after a couple of days. But the American staff were kindness itself, they were brilliant. I remember chatting up one gorgeous nurse, and thought I was doing rather well until she said: 'How old are you, kid?' I said: 'Twenty,' to which she replied, 'Gosh, I'd be kidnapping!' and she was off.

A BOAC Liberator flew us back to England, hugging the coast of Portugal, which was a neutral country. Flying in a civilian aircraft was brilliant: you got a little cardboard box with a boiled egg and bread and butter, and some jelly in a cup, which was luxury in those days.

Spooner, the engineer, who had been badly injured, recovered well. But Hi Walker, the pilot, didn't do any more operations after that, and went back to Canada where he was awarded a DSO.

I often think of Tony Farr, the young chap we lost. I should have taken the trouble to catch a train and go to see his wife, or at least written to her, but I was a young idiot and I'm sorry to say I didn't even think of it then. But so many died: I shared a hut with twenty aircrew, and every week several would go missing, and you just accepted it. If you'd got soft, you wouldn't have lasted. It's only now I think about them, these young men, just starting out in life . . .

I've just had my second pacemaker fitted at the age of eighty-eight, and it's given me a whole new lease of life. When I think back on that whole ditching episode, when I could so easily have died, I think: I'm a lucky devil, aren't I?!

WALTER 'BILL' COLLINGS

'Any Liverpool lads here . . . ?'

At the beginning of the war, I joined the LDV, the Local Defence Volunteers, which was later called the Home Guard; each night I'd go to the docks in Liverpool with my father to guard them, although we were there to protect them from looters just as much.

The bombs were raining down on to the docks, which was frightening, and a lot of people were getting killed, firemen especially. Then, when all the raids were over, there'd be no tramcars working, so we had to walk about an hour and a half to get to our house, which was near the Grand National course at Aintree.

Then the bombs started coming down at home; when the sirens went, mother used to go to a little cubbyhole underneath the stairs and my father would just sit on his own in the sitting room. One day, a bomb dropped that cleared an area of small flats next to us, and blew our front door in. I said to my father, 'I'll have to join the Army now.' I wanted to fight back, instead of sitting there when the bombs dropped.

Mother didn't want me to go, but eventually I joined a training battalion and they sent me up to Scotland. I was learning to use all sorts of weapons, but I ended up a sniper, because I was a good shot – since ten years old I'd been using a .410 shotgun to shoot rabbits. So I passed out as a sniper and was given a rifle with telescopic sights.

The Border Regiment, which I had joined, was based in Carlisle; we were all northern lads, no southerners at all, and a lot of us were from Liverpool. There's something about Liverpool that makes you feel unique. If you were in any gathering where there were a lot of troops, you could just listen and you'd know where the Liverpool lads were, so you headed towards them, because if you're Liverpool you're all friends, and you always knew that at any time you were in trouble, if you shouted, 'Any Liverpool lads here?' they'd come straight away.

In July of 1943 we were sent to North Africa, to start on the invasion of Sicily. The whole of our Border Regiment was going to be transported to Sicily in gliders. There were about ten of us in this glider; we took off in the very early morning, it wasn't yet daylight, and we were towed by American pilots using single-propeller biplanes called Wacos. As we came near to Sicily, the ack-ack fire was on, and our American pilot said he wouldn't go through the flak, so we had to come back out again and try another place to get in, which was all wrong. What our own British pilots did was to just go through a barrage, because you'd be very unlucky to get hit, and then you're through. But none of the Yanks would take us through; it wasn't just our pilot.

Two times there was flak, and two times our pilot pulled out, and then the third time we encountered flak he said, 'Cast off and good luck,' and let us down in the sea, nowhere near the island – we were about five miles out from Sicily when he released us.

Suddenly it was all quiet. As we were going down, I turned round to the lad next to me, Arkwright, to wish him good luck, and saw everyone throwing off their weapons, boots and everything that could weigh you down in the water. I had to more or less stand up on the seat to get my things off, and, as I was undoing them, we hit the water. It wasn't a big impact, the glider pilots did well, but my head went between the ribs of the fuselage and came up through the canvas, so I was the first out. After I pulled myself out of the glider, I reached back: I pulled Arkwright out, and there was a lad called Montford, and I pulled him out too.

We saw various parts of our glider disappearing under the water, the tail, the nose, the left wing, and then the right wing detached from the body, which disappeared under the water too. So all we had to cling on to was that wing. We moved along the wing and spread ourselves out along it. Where the flaps were situated on the back of the wing was a little crack, and our fingers could just about fit into that, so we all laid flat on the wing, with the waves washing over us, and just our fingers in that joint to hold us on. I could have been washed away at any time. What I haven't told you is that I couldn't swim.

I can still picture the lot of us strung out along that wing. Arkwright was on the left of me, and he couldn't swim a stroke either, same as me, and a lad named Morphy was on the right of me, and he kept grabbing hold of me, and, with his extra weight, I kept losing my grip, although fortunately Montford came along and helped to drag him off. Morphy could have killed me, with my not being able to swim.

Anyway, I couldn't see any chance of me getting to shore as we clung to our wing. I just accepted I was going to die. Also, the Italians on Sicily had searchlights and they were searching the water for fallen gliders – in fact, we were surrounded by other gliders that had been let loose by the Americans, although we couldn't see them because it was dark. As soon as the Italians found a glider, all their searchlights would focus on it, and then they would open fire and try to kill as many as they could. I did think of my parents then; my mother was a very emotional woman and I could imagine what she would go through when she heard I'd died. She would be devastated. My father had been in the First World War and he'd seen death, so I wasn't too worried about him.

I can remember it getting light the next morning, and

somebody shouted out, 'There's a boat over there.' I looked, and at first I couldn't see it; it was so far away there was no way we could signal to them. But Arkwright was at the end of the wing, and he was wearing a white vest, and one of the lads called out from further down the wing, 'Ask him to take his vest off, and we'll hold his legs,' the idea being he could then stand up and wave his vest. But Arkwright refused, because he didn't have anything else on. 'I'm not going to stand up like that,' he said. Can you imagine? It was so out of everything that he should worry about being naked in that situation, with nobody around except us. Everyone then shouted at him, and eventually he said, 'OK, I'll do it, but turn the other way.' He waved his vest, but shortly after he told us, 'I've had enough of this,' and down he went and put his vest back on.

As the day wore on, we saw a lot of small boats on their way to the island, and finally one landing craft came fairly close. The chap in charge stood up and shouted out to us, 'Sorry lads, pick you up when we get back.' He said he wasn't allowed to stop for us, because they had to get the troops they were carrying to the shore. We didn't mind a bit of a delay, he was going to come right back for us so we thought we were saved . . . but we never saw him again.

Many hours after that we saw a small frigate, and some of the lads waved to it and it started coming towards us; but the ship's propellers were sucking our plane down, and we were going under the water, but fortunately they saw that and stopped in time and lowered a boat. Montford noticed that our first-aid man, who was about a hundred yards away, was in difficulties, and as the rowing boat was coming towards us we told them to go to our friend first. There was this chap in a woolly hat in the rowing boat; he was a giant of a fellow, honestly. He stood up at the bow and dived straight into the sea, swam across to our friend – and I never saw anyone go so quick across the water – grabbed him by the scruff of his neck and got him into the rowing boat. He was a bloody hero. Then he came across to us, and got us all into the boat, and took us back to this frigate.

We weren't allowed to go down below at first – the sailors must have known what was going to happen ... This is very embarrassing, but we couldn't stop peeing. All the lads were the same, all the seawater and stuff was running out of our noses too, and we stayed on deck for about half an hour, just stood in a line. After a while we were all right, and then they let us go down below, wrapped us in blankets and brought us some hot chocolate, which had rum in it.

Eventually, we were transferred on to a ship called the *Marina del Pacifico*, which was a troopship, converted from a passenger ship, where they gave us clothes and food, and hot porridge. Turned out we were heading to Africa.

Later that day, I went up on deck and there was a young sailor walking along, and I asked him where we were going. As he was telling me, I said, 'Where are you from, Liverpool?' Well, it turns out he was from Fazakerley, and his aunt lived in the very street where I'm from. I took my watch off and asked him to give it to my parents as proof I was OK, because, although the water had finished it off, it was a special gift they had given me before I'd left home, and they would recognise it.

This young sailor got back to England, I was told later, and knocked on my parents' door. My father answered it, and the lad

248

said, 'This is your son's watch . . . ' and my dad immediately collapsed, assuming the worst. The idiot was supposed to tell my
parents right at the start that he'd seen me on his ship and I was
OK, and then give them the watch. But they got my dad right,
and told him I was fine.

Nothing seemed to worry me after the ditching, even though
I had two more crashes in a glider. One of the others, who was
married and had three children, couldn't get in a glider again. On
one occasion, when we were on our way to some skirmish, he
refused three times; he just couldn't get into that glider, and the
officers took him away for insubordination, and I never saw him
again.

When the lads from my battalion got back to North Africa,
they all arranged to go to the American camp one evening,
looking for these pilots who had been towing our gliders.
And there was heck to pay: they beat up all the pilots they
could find. I wasn't there, but I was told about it when I got
back, but actually, I think if I'd had a gun I would have shot
them. Because of those pilots, five to six hundred of our lads
were killed or drowned during the invasion of Sicily. They
should have gone through the flak: they had to take the
chance, just as we had to take the chance. If they had just
gone straight through the flak, they would have been out and
away, but so many of these American pilots wouldn't go
through, and in a glider we were dependent on the towing
aircraft pilot.

I couldn't swim then, and I still can't swim, and I'm ninety, so
I reckon I'm not going to learn any time in the future now. I
tried swimming when my children were growing up; I went in

as far as my legs, but I couldn't do it, I had to go out. You might not believe this, but I won't go under a shower either, because of the water going over my head all the time, it brings back too many memories.

JOHN PROUT

'Beaufighters be damned, those are Junkers 88s . . . '

We were very patriotic, we were doing it for King and Country, and of course we knew about the horrors the Germans were inflicting, the extermination of the Jews was just beginning, and we just had to get rid of Hitler, and that was that.

In early 1942 I was in the Devonshire Regiment, guarding the east coast of England, waiting for a German invasion which never came, and it was getting a bit boring so I thought I would like to do something more exciting. First of all I volunteered for the Tank Corps, but didn't get a reply. Then I thought Airborne Forces sounded interesting, so I put down for that; I went for an interview, and they said, 'What are you going to volunteer for? Parachutists or Glider Forces?' I wasn't keen on jumping out of aeroplanes, so I said, 'Gliders,' and they immediately said, 'Fighter Pilot Regiment,' and within a week I was called for an aircrew medical, which I had on my twenty-first birthday, 24 June 1942

I went home, to Totnes in Devon, and while I was at home I got a call to report to the headquarters of the Glider Pilot Regiment on Salisbury Plain, so then I went into training as a glider pilot. We were organised just like an infantry unit, and it was a very tough regiment; we had Guards officers, who were very strict disciplinarians, running us all over the countryside to improve our fitness. But I wasn't there very long when I was sent to flying training school at Shillingford in Oxfordshire, where a lot of RAF trainees were, because we all had to learn to fly Tiger Moths to start with. I remember my first lesson. The instructor asked if I liked flying and I told him I had never been in an aeroplane. 'What?!' he said. 'You have volunteered as a pilot and never been in an aeroplane before?' But I don't think that was so unusual in those days.

It was all great fun. I could loop the loop, and did lots of things we weren't supposed to do, like fly over the fields in the countryside, and if I saw a rabbit I would try to bounce my wheels on top of it, and the farmers ploughing with their horses would shake their fists at us.

Three months of training as an aircraft pilot and then we were sent to glider training school near Cheltenham, and learned to fly small gliders. We did two months on the Hotspurs, which were eight-seaters, made of plywood; well, all gliders were made of plywood. You were attached by a long rope to the towing aircraft; the glider had to take off before the towing aircraft, but hold it down to a couple of feet off the ground, because, if the towing aircraft got off before the glider, the glider pulled its tail down and the towing aircraft would stall.

We then transferred to Brize Norton where we learned to fly the larger gliders, the Horsas, which carried thirty people.

We used to love to frighten the RAF pilots around Brize Norton in our Horsas. We would invite them to come up as passengers; these gliders had enormous flaps and you could take the glider up to eight hundred feet, right above the edge of the runway of the aerodrome, put on full flap and then stall deliberately, and you'd come down vertically, hanging on the flaps, and then pull out about thirty feet from the ground, by which time the RAF passengers were terrified. Well, we were young and cheeky.

The idea was for us to carry troops to Europe for an invasion. A Horsa glider could land anywhere, a cornfield, or meadow, which is what we did in Normandy when we landed.

Meanwhile, there had been a glider-borne invasion of Sicily where they had used some Horsas, but mostly they used little American gliders called Wacos, which the British called Hadrians. I wasn't involved in that one, but we had inexperienced American pilots towing the gliders into Sicily, and when the Americans got near the coast they saw the anti-aircraft fire, panicked and just dropped the gliders into the sea – we lost two to three hundred men like that – they were simply drowned. Until recent years it was never published what the Americans had done, but it was common knowledge in the regiment. After the Sicily invasion the Americans threw a party for their glider pilots at their aerodrome, and the pilots all had to be frisked for knives and guns before they went in because they were so furious with the Yanks.

In August 1942 I was transferred to Herne, near Bournemouth, and told we had a job to ferry gliders from England out to North Africa. Nobody had ever before flown a glider for ten hours on tow, so we had a trial flight, flying round and round England for ten hours to see if any problems occurred. One bunch went before my lot, and there had been quite a number of losses one way or another, people coming down in the sea, shot down, or engine failure.

We were the second contingent; our op was called Elaborate. We had to ferry these guys and land them just outside Rabat in Morocco, stay a couple of nights there and then go on and fly another six hours to a place called Sousse, in Tunisia, leave the glider there and come back to England in the towing aircraft. Well, I did that successfully once, and I was doing it a second time when my ditching story begins.

We took the glider and the Halifax down to Portreath in north Cornwall, and then at six o' clock in the morning, 18 September 1943, off we went on our trip to North Africa. The towing air-craft was piloted by my very good friend Gerry Norman, and there were three of us in the plane, myself and Sergeant Peter Hill and Sergeant Harry Flynn, who were the first and second pilots at the controls.

It is very hard physical work to hold the glider in position at the speed the Halifax is flying, because a glider is essentially designed to fly very gently at about sixty miles an hour, and the towing aircraft towed us at 140 miles an hour, which makes the controls very difficult to operate, not to say physically arduous, because you had to hold position in relation to the towing aircraft, and if you didn't you would probably go down, cause the towing aircraft to stall and there would be a crash.

Nothing very eventful happened at first. We had been told we would have a Beaufighter escort, and at about ten o'clock in the morning Harry Flynn looked out and said, 'Oh look, there's our Beaufighter escort.' But my aircraft recognition was better than his. I looked at him and said, 'Beaufighters be damned, those are Junkers 88s.' Both planes were twin-engine single monoplanes, of course, but the Beaufighter engine was further forward, so it stuck out in front of the nose of the aircraft.

Anyway, right on cue, tracer bullets started coming across our nose, but didn't hit us, fortunately. I said to Peter Hill, who was actually flying the glider at the time, 'Pull off,' in other words release the plane. We had an agreement with the pilot of the towing aircraft that if we were attacked we would release and leave him alone, and go down into the sea, because the Halifax couldn't possibly manoeuvre with us on its back.

So that's what we did, and then we were in free flight and Peter Hill put us gently down in the sea: a very good bit of piloting, not sure I could have done so well.

You had to hack a hole in the fuselage with an axe to get to the escape hatch, and there was a rubber dinghy in a big container, and we got into our dinghy. But then the Germans came back, and one

Junkers 88 came down and fired at us. I remember Harry saying, 'Shall we get out into the water?' and I said, 'What the hell for, we might get wet!' But I really thought this was the end. And then the next plane came along, but it didn't fire, and then all eight of them came down, but they didn't fire either; I don't know why, but I suspect that the German squadron commander probably said to his people, 'No, hold your fire', because it was contrary to the general ethics of flying to shoot at people in the water, or when they were hanging on their parachutes. Anyway, they didn't shoot again and left us. Actually, what we later learned was that they had gone off and tried to shoot down our towing Halifax, and failed. How eight of them could fail to shoot down a single Halifax I don't know, but the Halifax had actually managed to get into the clouds and get away, which is why they all came back to us.

I never met him, but I wrote to and received letters from the German commander, who died in 1984. There was a German sergeant called Hommel, who actually got the credit for shooting us down, and I was shown his logbook entry, which says: 'Just flying around the Bay of Biscay, seeing what there was. We met one Halifax and a transport glider, a Horsa, and shot it down. Good hunting.'

Anyway, Harry Flynn said, 'Shall we swim for it?' and I said 'No' as we were miles from land and it was a very rough sea. We were in the dinghy for about twelve hours and the water was coming over the side, and we had to bail out every now and again with a little bucket. I don't know if you have ever been in a rubber dinghy, but where you sit sinks down and all the water that came in at the side accumulated around our backsides, which got rather wet.

It is amazing, but you do get extremely lethargic in these situations. We kept saying, 'We have got to bail this dinghy out,' and we would think about it for a while, and then, half an hour later, 'Come on, we are going to bail the water out ...' And eventually we would, but it took a lot of time to actually make ourselves do it.

We were two hundred miles from land in a rough sea out in the Bay of Biscay in a dinghy. I did think this was the end, aged twenty-two. Well, it happened to a lot of other people, so you knew it was quite likely it would happen to you. The likelihood of a lieutenant surviving was pretty low.

Pete Hill and I were quite relaxed. I remember Flynn said at one point, 'If I get away from this, I'm never going to fly again.' And I don't think he ever did fly again.

We were watching out for aircraft flying over, and we saw a Liberator go at quite a distance. In the box was a flare pistol and I tried to get it out quickly, but I opened the wrong end of the box and by the time I got it out the plane had gone. And then a Sunderland came over, a bit nearer than the Liberator. This time we fired the flare, but he didn't see us. And then he came back very close to us, so I fired the Very pistol, and he saw us this time and dropped floating flares around us and also a big canister of food. We already had a supply of food in the dinghy, but we didn't know how long we would be there; indeed, some friends of ours in the squadron had been adrift for twelve days in a dinghy on the previous operation, so we thought it best to retrieve this food.

The canister was floating just about a hundred yards from us, and there were paddles in the dinghy, but a dinghy is round and trying to get two people to paddle to where something is float-ing is very difficult. It actually took us an hour or so to get to the food.

Just after it got dark, we heard an aircraft coming, and this air-craft circled over and renewed the supply of float flares around us. Then he went off.

We had sort of settled down for the night, but after a while we could hear the sound of a ship's engines. I didn't want to waste my flares, so I waited until the ship was pretty close and then I fired the flare again, and the ship stopped and came alongside – although I was in trouble with the captain of the ship: 'Why did you wait so bloody long with your flare?' he said. 'We nearly ran you down!' Nevertheless, they hauled us over the side and we spent a week on board the ship, HMS *Crane*.

The captain had been with a flotilla, looking for U-boats, and a message had got through to him that we had come down in the sea, and he was detached from the rest of the flotilla to go and look for us. I don't think he was too pleased being out on his own; he was certainly jumpy about stopping, because a British ship standing still in the Bay of Biscay is a bit of a sitting target for a U-boat. I was very thankful we never saw any U-boats. I'd had enough of Germans by that time.

I was put into the first lieutenant's cabin and slept up in the forward cabin, and the two sergeants went to sleep in hammocks with the petty officers. There wasn't much for us to do then, but the medical officer on the boat had very little to do himself, and he and I would sit up on top in the sunshine and chat and drink. Well, there was always a drink on offer, because the Royal Navy had alcohol on board in those days.

Crane dropped us at Plymouth and we got someone to take us to the airport, and I phoned our station at Herne and spoke to the duty officer. 'Please will you send an aircraft down to Plymouth to fetch us?' He didn't want to at first, and I said, 'Bloody hell, man, we have just been shot down, so you had better find an aircraft to come and fetch us right away.' So they sent a twin-engined Oxford down to Plymouth to pick us up and take us back to Herne.

I don't remember any particular celebration when we got back to the mess, just, 'Ah, Johnny, there you are!'

Subsequently I went on to fly even larger gliders, the Hamilcars, which could carry a tank. They were the biggest aircraft flying at that time, with a wingspan of 110 feet, which was a lot then but nothing now.

I flew one of those into Normandy on D-Day, when we were carrying a tank, plus the crew of the tank. We flew over about five o'clock in the afternoon on D-Day, 6 June 1944. It was a textbook operation; we landed in the field exactly where we had planned to land. We then formed up as a company of infantry with all the pilots, dug ourselves in on the edge of a field and waited for the Germans to come – which they didn't. The next morning they said, 'Right, the ground troops have caught up with us, and we can go back,' because we were under instructions to return to England as soon as possible, to be ready for the next operation. And so we started to make our way back.

There were masses of bodies on the beach all piled up, with several bulldozers working full time getting rid of them, but where we were, close to the front, they hadn't had time to remove all the bodies. Lying at the side of the road, right where we were walking, was a dead German soldier, about seventeen years old, just a boy, really, because the Germans had all their best troops fighting on the Russian front, so they used youngsters and old men to defend the French coast. And that scene epitomises for me the reality of war. This dead boy was lying there, and his eyes were open, and his eyeballs were covered in dust. And I have never stopped thinking of that boy ever since then: some poor mother was going to hear quite soon that her seventeen-year-old son had been killed in Normandy and was never coming back.

I've been very lucky all my life. I had the good fortune of being born in Devon, I had a wonderful marriage, although I'm now a widower, and I've been lucky enough to see my ninetieth birthday, and the completion of my first ninety years.

I didn't have to endure the horrors that people had in the First World War, no sitting in the trenches or going over the top. I mean, it was not a pleasure to sit in the sea, but nobody was wounded, there was no real suffering.

Actually, I thoroughly enjoyed my six years in the Army. Those were some of the happiest years of my life: carefree, provided for, we lived in comfort, and when I became a glider pilot we were on aircrew rations, and we got extra rations of eggs and orange juice, which was bliss, really.

DOUG CANNING

I wanted to get to Stevenage ...

I'd never been in a plane before, but I always had an ambition
to fly so I volunteered to join the RAF. I had a very long interview, and then had to go back three times. There were general
knowledge questions: who was the Prime Minister? Who was the
minister for war? And then a medical, which seemed to go on for
ever.

Anyway, I passed, and we went down to Newquay to do our

training; we did maths and navigation and played a lot of hockey on the beach. My instructor was Russian and I found him quite difficult to understand at first, and frequently had to ask him to repeat what he was saying. Our first flight, which was in a Tiger Moth, I remember he said: 'Hold the joystick like there's a little fly on it, you don't want to kill the little fly!' which was a funny way of putting it.

After Newquay, we went to Scotland where we did more training, and a lot of flying on Wellingtons and Wimpy 10s, Beauforts, which were clumsy old things, and then the Avro Anson, which was very hot to fly in – we used to call it the Flying Greenhouse. I liked the Sterling most of all, a heavy bomber that had been developed from the Sunderland flying boat, and was very steady.

We were in a Sterling when we ditched. We were a crew of seven who had been together some time. My particular friends were the bomb aimer, Percy Brett, who later crashed in Yugoslavia and died, and the mid-upper gunner, who was a young Canadian of about seventeen who had just joined our crew, a very funny chap called David, but for some reason was known as Mushy – that's what he was called at home in Canada – Mushy Moore. I corresponded with him for a long time after the war. The rear gunner was a chap called Stanley, who was older than the rest of us, in his thirties I think, which seemed quite old to us at the time.

It was a nice, sunny day in August 1942, a lovely day in fact, and we were not expecting any more flying that day, but suddenly we were called to the Briefing Room and told we were to go on a sea search for a crew that had gone down off the Danish coast the night before. We were warned to keep a watch out, because we were likely to be picked up by the Germans, but we went up and down the Danish coast for five or six hours, looking for this dinghy, but all we saw were lots of little Danish fishing boats, and even though we were flying quite low, four hundred feet, and sometimes lower, it was quite difficult to see anything, because the sea was choppy.

Suddenly, with no warning at all, the outer starboard engine went, then the inner starboard cut out, and same again on the port side. The skipper shouted, 'The engines have cut!' And when the third one went, he shouted, 'Dinghy stations.' We'll never know what happened, but there wasn't anything we could do at that height, and within a couple of minutes we were down in the water: there was one terrific bang, a hell of a noise, and the aircraft actually broke in half, right down the middle. I remember it getting very dark and black under the water, and I had to clamber to the back of the aircraft after it hit the water. By the time I bobbed up to the surface, I could see the dinghy under the wing, but I couldn't get in – it's difficult to get up the sides of a dinghy – but the rest of the crew dragged me aboard. Everyone was there except the rear gunner, Stanley, who was missing. We bobbed around awhile, and then someone shouted: '*There* he is . . . ' He was some distance away, sitting on the tail of the aircraft, which had broken off, and he was hopping mad – it isn't printable what he was saying – because we hadn't rescued him before. Anyway, we paddled towards the tail with our hands, and eventually pulled him aboard the dinghy.

By then a fishing boat called the *Connie* was coming towards us. We were glad to be picked up, but we also wondered whether we should do something about trying to escape. When we asked the crew where we were going, they said, 'No problem, we'll evade the Germans, and take you around the north of Denmark and into Sweden.' We didn't have much option but to trust them. They hauled our dinghy on to their deck – on reflection, if they were going to take us to Sweden they would have hidden it, because the Germans would have been suspicious of a dinghy – anyway, we were on the boat a couple of hours before we got into port at Esjberg. Then, within seconds of coming into dock, two German soldiers boarded the ship with guns and shouted for us to get off. So it seems our 'saviours' were German sympathisers.

In fact, I've been to Esbjerg since. I went down with my wife in our caravan. I wanted to meet that captain to find out whether he intended to take us to Sweden or not. We talked to someone who said he knew the skipper of the boat that picked us up, but he had drowned. He'd come home drunk one night and fallen into the sea. So I'll never know now . . .

The Germans weren't very friendly. They took us into a small room in a building on the side of the docks, and just left us there all night, with someone sitting at the door. There were no beds, no mattresses, nothing. I remember them saying before they left us: 'For you, the war is over. It's a long way to Tipperary . . .' which seemed a bit of a non-sequitur, but I think was the only English they knew. We discussed among ourselves how we could escape, but there wasn't much we could do.

The next day, the Germans brought a piece of black bread and a lump of meat, and we were marched along the road and put onto a tram in to town. The town was very busy, there were a lot of people about, and they were all shouting insults at us; I didn't know very much German then, but I got the gist of it.

From there we were taken to the station and locked into a cattle truck for three days, which was a horrible journey. We were sitting on the floor the whole time, we had nothing to lie on, and we had just this one piece of meat and some bread, and water the guards fetched for us. The truck was enclosed, there were no windows, but we could see through cracks in the walls, and sometimes, if the train stopped, the guards would open the door and sit outside with a gun resting on their knees. We had no idea where we were going, but the thoughts were always: 'How can we escape?'

We arrived at the Gestapo building in Frankfurt, and I was put in solitary confinement. There was a mattress on the floor which was infested with fleas, and when I complained to the interrogator, he said: 'I expect it's your American friends who left them ... ' The interrogator spoke perfect English. In fact, he'd lived in London before the war and he was very courteous; he offered me cigarettes and was quite pleasant, really. In his room was a huge map on the wall with flags dotted over it, which represented different RAF stations. I was interrogated three or four times and it was always the same: 'Where have you come from? Where were you going? What sort of aircraft were you in?' and I gave only my name, rank and number.

From there we were taken to another part of the building where there were dozens and dozens of aircrew – although I had an idea that some of them were Germans who were planted there in order to overhear our conversations – I think that's where they got a lot of their information from.

We were taken again in a cattle truck down to Stalag IV-B, which was on the River Elbe not far from Dresden. That also took a few days, and we were often shunted off to side railings for traffic to come through. I don't think we were top priority at all.

Stalag IV-B was pretty grim; it was primarily a Russian camp, and there were thousands of Russians there, and they were in a terrible state, half starved, filthy dirty and dressed in ragged clothes.

When we arrived, we were herded into one room where our hair was shaved, and all our clothes taken away, and we were given a jab – there'd been an attack of typhoid in the camp, and hundreds of Russians had died. The disease had spread to the German village nearby, and people there were dying from it, so they were very keen for it not to happen again. We were taken into a shower room where there were lots and lots of shower-heads in the ceiling – we didn't know about the gas ovens then, if we had we might have been more alarmed. We just stood under these jets of water, there was no soap or towels, and they switched off the water eventually and pumped in hot air, which dried us.

We were put into large wooden huts in batches of two hundred, with bunks three tiers high on each side. We were the first RAF to be taken there – all the special RAF camps were full up by then. We met the Russians when we went on parade the next morning, and later on, if any of our chaps wanted to escape, we'd get a Russian to come and stand in to make up the numbers, which would give the person a chance to get away.

Our Red Cross parcels didn't come through for several months, so we were completely dependent on German rations, which weren't very good. I was hungry all the time. At about 11 a.m., two of us would go to the kitchen for a big bucket of turnip or swede soup, and two hundred grams of bread each, which was our ration for the day. You'd try to hang back a bit in the line getting your soup, because if you got to the very end of the queue you might get a piece of meat in it.

Eventually Red Cross parcels came for us. It wasn't always one each – sometimes you shared it between four or five others, depending on how many had come through – but we were very grateful to the Red Cross. I think they saved our lives.

Once we'd finished with our food parcels, we dumped the tins into this big pit, and I remember seeing Russians pulling these old tins out and putting their hands deep inside them, and then sucking their fingers, because they were so hungry.

Later on, the Red Cross sent books, and games as well, and footballs too. It was quite a big compound, so we had space for a kickaround, and we played against each other, and when eventually they brought in other nationals as prisoners of war we had international games. I don't think any of us were particularly good; we didn't have enough energy from our diet for one thing, but it passed the time. Some people organised classes of various kinds in the camp, language classes mainly. I learned quite a lot of German, and I read lots of books. Most of them were about South America, for some odd reason, and the worst titles they sent were cookery books: all those lovely dishes of food . . .

The worst part of being a prisoner of war was not knowing how long we would be there; we obviously had no idea how long the war was going to go on. The German propaganda machine used to send out a newspaper in English every month round the camp to say how well the war was going for them – although we didn't believe it, of course.

I was in the camp just under two years in all. I got scarlet fever while I was there, but a South African doctor who was also prisoner got me through it. I felt so helpless, not being able to continue to fight, and I planned an escape with an English friend at one point. We'd noticed that to the left of the main gate there was a wire with a large space in the middle. We didn't have much to do with the French, we didn't trust them: for one reason, the French prisoners were allowed out on working parties without escorts of any sort. They were clearly on friendly terms with the Germans. Anyway, we thought we'd borrow some French clothes, get near that gap in the wire as they came through, then, when we were level, quickly join in the back of the line. But for various reasons we didn't do it . . .

For weeks we could hear the approach of the Russians, the sky would be lit up at night with explosions, which were getting closer and closer. Then, one night, there was one hell of a noise and the Germans just left us in the camp and scarpered. The Russians told us if we wanted to leave we could walk back with them via Moscow, or something daft like that. They tied any German guards they found on to the back of their vehicles and dragged them along the ground. They were pitiless.

We were told to forage for food, so we went round to German houses and picked up whatever we could. Most of the Germans had fled anyway, and when we looked in their cellars we found all sorts of food they'd hoarded. We went to one place where the farmer had a pen of chickens and we asked him if we could have one, so he got hold of a chicken and chopped its head off. We took it back to the camp, made a fire with some of the wood we'd collected and cooked it. It was the first decent thing we'd had to eat in a long time, and I can still remember that chicken. Very good it was too.

We left the camp, clambered across a bridge that had been partially blown up and walked for several days towards Halle, where we'd heard there were Allied troops. When we got there we found empty houses we could stay in, although most of the bigger, more prosperous homes had been ransacked by the Russians. Eventually, the Americans came along on one of their patrols and picked us up. They were very friendly, and took us back to their camp and gave us some food, along with white bread, which we hadn't tasted for years. They flew us back to Brussels in a Dakota, and we spent the night there before flying back to England where we were given indefinite leave.

I wanted to get to Stevenage, which is about twenty-eight miles down the line from London, but I fell asleep on the train and passed Stevenage, and then had to catch a train back again. I got on that train, and then went to sleep again, and didn't wake up until Hatfield, so I had to turn around again to get back to Stevenage. I must have been exhausted.

When I finally got to Stevenage, I took a bus down to Walkern, the village where I lived with my parents before I went to war. I had phoned up my family to say I was on my way, and they were waiting for me. The house was decorated with flags flying and 'Welcome Home Doug' banners, and all the rest of it. My mother was very pleased to see me. I had a brother who was out in Burma at that time, and another brother in the RAF. My third brother had been killed; he worked in the engine room on a destroyer and had volunteered to go ashore to fight. He was buried at the military cemetery in Oran in Algeria.

Being home was very weird at first. I kept dreaming I was still in the camp, then I'd wake up and find I wasn't. That went on for an awful long time. One thing we didn't get much of in the camp was green vegetables or salad, and I consumed so much of it once I was home I made myself ill.

We were all expecting to go out to the Far East and continue the war, but after the atomic bombs they started demobbing almost immediately. My wife-to-be, Clarice, was also in the RAF, and we got engaged when she got demobbed and married a couple of months afterwards. And we're still happily married now and I turned ninety two days ago.

BRIAN JONES

'Get on to the Prudential ... '

I was brought up in a mining village near Doncaster; my father was a coal miner, as was his father and grandfather. But I was dead keen about the sea, and I remember in 1947, when I'd be coming up fourteen, I spent a fortnight with my auntie in Hull, and used all my time wandering around the docks, and whenever I saw a sailor in his uniform I used to be right envious.

Anyway, I was determined I was going to be a sailor, and I was fifteen when I joined the Navy, and my parents were chuffed to nuts I wasn't going down the pit.

The first time I went on a plane was when I was stationed at HMS *Daedalus*, which was a Navy air station in Lee-on-Solent, Hampshire, and we flew around the Isle of Wight, and I didn't like it very much.

In 1958, I got a draft to Ceylon for two years, where I was a telegraphist. Coming back to the UK, the first stop in our journey was Gan, an island in the Maldives, in the Indian Ocean.

We were in a Hastings, which was called the 'flying tractor' because it rattled so much, and, also, the seats faced backwards in them, so you saw where you'd been, not where you were going – they were weird things, they were. Well, we were approaching Gan, and the conditions were terrible: there was a huge tropical storm raging outside, thunder and lightning, the rain lashing down, and it was pitch-black, not even a sliver of moon. We came in to land, and on the first attempt the pilot landed too far up the runway, took off again and did another circuit, and then literally set the plane down two or three minutes later, and, God, that was a bumpy landing, and noisy too.

Anyway, I stood up when we stopped, put my hat on, folded my raincoat over my arm and picked up my little bag, ready to disembark, until this flight sergeant down the aisle noticed me, and said, 'You don't need all that, mate, put *this* on', and thrust a life jacket in my arm. And that was my first inkling as to what had happened. I hadn't realised we had ditched.

Suddenly, the water rushed in above our waists, although by this time I had my life jacket on, and I followed everybody up to the door where life rafts were already waiting. We had to swim towards the boats, though, and the waves were so rough I had the impression I was swimming uphill. But I thought, I can make this no problem, the water is so warm; well, we were practically on the equator.

There were about twenty people on the plane. Everybody was RAF, apart from me and one Royal Marine – 'crab fats' we used to call them. The life rafts were big round things, and a bit difficult to get into, but this Royal Marine was a big fella and he just grabbed hold of me and yanked me in. He and I then helped the others get in, and there were about ten of us in our life raft, and another life raft with the same number again. I remember sitting in the sea looking at our aeroplane, and it was as steady as a rock for about twenty minutes, and then it started sinking, and we watched it go down and all the lights were still on inside.

The sea was quite rough, and most of the RAF blokes were being violently seasick, but we had an RAF officer on our life raft who said, 'Let's have a singsong.' Well, we had only been in the water less than an hour. I reckon he'd seen too many Hollywood films.

Anyway, I got into trouble because I sang the naval version of 'The Eton Boating Song', which is rather rude. The first verse goes: 'Jolly fine weather for boating, Won't you come for a ride in my punt, But if you don't want to go boating, You can poke my punt up your . . . ' And then the chorus goes, 'We'll all pull together, Our bollocks between our knees,' etc. I hadn't got halfway through when this officer said, 'Er, Jones, we don't sing that type of song here.' So I lost interest then.

Anyway, by this time we could see there was a Shackleton out looking for us, and I remember thinking, 'Oh, he'll find us in a bit, we'll be all right.' And then the Shackleton found us, and began dropping flares, and these RAF air-sea rescue boats came and hauled us on board a Royal Navy frigate.

Next morning we were waiting for this plane to come in from Singapore to continue the journey, and they said, 'Anybody who doesn't want to get on it needn't, we'll understand.' And one of the RAF blokes pulled out.

I didn't know this at the time, but when we ditched they sent my wife a telegram, saying, 'The plane has crashed; no survivors . . . ' Of course it should have read: 'The plane has crashed; no survivors as yet . . . ' My dear mother-in-law read it, and immediately said, 'He's dead. Get on to the Prudential.' But my wife had a feeling I wasn't dead, and she left Yorkshire and went down to the naval barracks in Portsmouth. When she got there, she explained who she was, and this officer said to her, 'Oh, I'm so sorry, Mrs Jones . . . ' and she fainted clean away. But what he was going on to say was, 'I'm so sorry, Mrs Jones, that telegram should have said, "as yet".'

Eventually we flew to Karachi in a Britannia, one of old turbo-prop four-engine turbos – the 'Whispering Giant' was the nickname for them. But almost as soon as the aeroplane took off, it started flying round in circles and I looked out and saw all this stuff coming out of the wings. Hey up, something's wrong again, I thought. And then the pilot came on and said, 'We have a problem, we're going to have to go back to Karachi, but we'll have to empty the fuel tanks first.' Crikey, I thought, I'm never going to get home. And then I was really frightened, because the other accident had happened so quickly, plus I never really knew what was happening, so I never felt any fear. Anyway, all the emergency vehicles were waiting at the end of the runway as we came in to land, and as we touched down they all took off after us. But we landed OK, no problem. It turned out that a bolt had sheared and got trapped in the mechanism.

They had to send to Bahrain to get the spare part, so then we had a day in the airport lounge in Karachi, which is a godawful place. We finally left there, and landed at a big RAF base in Cyprus, where we had a big fry-up of egg, fried bread and chips; oh, what a greasy mess that meal was. They teach chefs now; in those days it was 'You're a chef now, cook something' kind of thing, but we ate it because we were starving.

A few years back I was stricken with bowel cancer, but they caught it in time and I had the operation, and everything's all right. But I remember talking to my youngest son about it, and he said, 'Well, it would have been all right if you had died.'

'What do you mean?' I asked.

He said, 'Don't get me wrong, Dad, I don't want you to die, but you've had an interesting life, you've even survived a plane crash, and not many people can say that, can they?' And I thought, He's right, it's quite unique what happened to me.

And now I think of my ditching as a badge of honour, and I'm really quite proud to be a member of the Goldfish Club. Mind you, we get a quarterly magazine in the Goldfish Club, and I look at some of these obituaries, and they'll say, 'He was shot down by two Messerschmitts,' or you read that one of them had been floating around the ocean for three or four days before he got picked up, and I think: for crying out loud, I'm in the same company as these people. Mine was a mere sideshow compared to what they went through.

Anyway, my ditching didn't put me off flying: I didn't like flying before then. We have spent a lot of our holidays abroad, especially Spain, and I still have to have a good couple of slugs of brandy before I get on the aeroplane, in fact sometimes three.

ARTHUR BREEZE

The loneliest sound in the world . . .

The date is chiselled in my mind. It was the afternoon of 19 October 1953. It was a nice day, bright blue sky, not much cloud, and we'd had an uneventful morning. Then, in a moment, the plane was spinning out of control, it crashed explosively into the sea, along with my friend and co-pilot, and suddenly I was in the water on my own. This terrible emptiness was highlighted by the sound of waves rolling relentlessly along. That scene has stayed with me ever since then, and it still really gets to me because it's so sad. I never felt so alone. It upsets me every time I think about it, and it always makes me weep.

I was a member of 25 Squadron at West Malling in Kent; we were the night-fighter force for the defence of south-east England, and our job was to stop anything hostile coming in at night. We flew Vampires, a single-engine jet fighter. The big problem was getting in and out of them: there was only a tiny hatch in the roof, so the ground crew stuck a little ladder along-side and the navigator got in first, then the pilot. You could only get in or out with help from ground crew.

We were always working on PIs, practice interceptions – they were our life. Two Vampires would go off as a pair then, when we'd picked up the other aeroplane on the radar, we'd strike a converging course and then get ourselves in a position behind it. A Vampire has a short-range pick-up compared to modern radar; if we were lucky we'd pick up the target when it was two or three miles away. The idea then was to track the target until the pilot was satisfied he was in a position to identify it as enemy aircraft, and 'shoot' it down.

On this particular day, we broke port and pulled alongside the target aeroplane, which was another Vampire from our squadron. We then waited there for the next interception, when we would be the target, and another airplane could practise on us.

I was flying with John Digman-White. I'd trained with Diddy, we'd gone through the OCU together, arrived on the squadron together and flew together most of the time. John had been an airman during the war; he was twenty-seven, so older than most of us, although the truth is, at twenty-one, I was getting a little bit long in the tooth myself; most people on the squadron were eighteen or nineteen. He was a nice chap, we got on extremely well; he 'fathered' me a little bit, looked after me and stopped me from doing all the stupid things you do when you're young, like getting drunk in the pub. We even shared a room for about four months, until he got married and moved out.

We had already done one sortie that morning, and at half-past two we took off again for the afternoon session. There was cloud around, but we were flying above it, so to us it was a nice day. We carried out two or three practice interceptions, and at about 3.30 we began our last PI. We'd been airborne about fifty minutes when we pulled alongside at about twenty thousand feet. Our target was on our right, and we turned across each other, which was no real problem because we could still see each other. But then I heard Diddy White say: 'Oh, he's going down too ...' which meant the other pilot was descending to cross us. We'd already half initiated a descent, so Diddy eased the stick back to go over the top of him, and that was when all hell broke loose, because suddenly our aeroplane flipped into a complete roll; the nose shot up into the air until we were almost vertical, and then it just dropped straight into a spin. 'Get out!' Diddy said. There was no, 'Put on parachutes, prepare to abandon aircraft,' or anything like that, it was just 'GET OUT!' I jettisoned the hood, disconnected the seat harness and turned on the oxygen. And then, just before I got rid of the intercom, I heard the other pilot shouting, 'Jettison your tanks! Jettison your tanks!' and Diddy replying, 'They won't go!'

I turned to go over the side of the aeroplane, and I was pushing with my harness, trying to get out, but there was something catching at the back of the parachute pack and I couldn't get out. Suddenly, a strong arm just shoved me out, and I was out in the clear, and found myself on my back, falling.

I have no idea what height we were at that point, but we still had cloud; the next thing was to go for the D-ring, but when I pulled nothing happened. I tried again, then looked, and realised it had moved virtually under my armpit. I pulled it again, and it seemed an eternity before the pilot chute, a tiny piece of fabric the size of a sixpence, was suddenly fluttering between my legs, and a moment later I was hanging on the main parachute. I could see the town of Deal fourteen miles away, bathed in sunlight, and way, way below me, the aeroplane spiralling down. And then there was an almighty CRASH as it hit the sea. I was just entering cloud at that point, but when I broke through I could see the sea had changed to a bright green where the aeroplane had smashed into it, and a big patch of ripples fanning out from it, and then I drifted well away.

Just as I hit the water, the wind tipped my parachute and I finished with the parachute dragging me backwards along the surface of the water. I'd thought the North Sea in mid-October was not going to be nice, but I was amazed how warm the sea felt. It didn't take long before I was in the dinghy with my little emergency pack, but I would have to say the sound of the sea, and the whine of the Vampire engine of our practice partner above me, was the loneliest sound in the world. It's a scene that has never left me, and it still upsets me whenever I think about it.

I knew straight away that Diddy had gone. There's no way he could have survived. For one thing, he wouldn't have actually been able to get out of the plane on his own. We'd lost quite a few people on the station; you'd speak to a bloke one night in the bar, then he would go off on a night trip and you wouldn't see him ever again, although of course it wasn't as frequent as it was during the war with the Lancasters and Spitfires. But we lost a crew from 85 Squadron on an exercise in June '53, then we lost Diddy, and then three weeks later another bloke bailed out and crashed into the sea, and was washed up a fortnight later.

Before long I was joined by four Meteor 8s, and weaving in between them was an American Albatross, an amphibious flying boat. I thought the Albatross might have picked me up, but all he did was fly over me and sling out some sea marker. I found out later he was looking for the pilot, which was pointless; the aeroplane had been in an uncontrollable spin. There was no control over it at all.

It's also possible that Diddy had the same problem with his harness as I did, but with no one left to give him a shove there was no way he would get out . . . I am probably the only person ever to survive getting out of a Vampire NF.10.

After a couple of hours, the *Sledgwick*, a five-thousand-ton Danish cargo ship on its way to Rotterdam, pulled alongside; the crew dropped a ladder down and I climbed up. The second mate had been a pilot on a Spitfire squadron during the war and he looked after me very well; he stripped my clothes off me and gave me a glass of whisky and a cigarette. I don't know which I finished first, but they had both gone by the time I hit the shower. When we arrived at Rotterdam the next morning, my clothes were washed and dried and in a neat little bundle.

Then it all got a little bit frustrating. The Dutch police came to the boat at 7.30 the next morning, wanting to know why I was in the country without prior arrangement. So I told them my story, and they rang the British Consulate in Rotterdam from their phone. I said: 'I am Pilot Officer Breeze, and I've arrived here inadvertently,' only to be told: 'Don't bother us now, old chap, we don't open until nine.'

So the police took me down to the Consulate, and I was shipped through four different offices before anyone would see me. I eventually ended up at the Department for Distressed Seamen, where two blokes asked me for my story again. I told them I wanted to get back to England, so they talked to the Air

Attaché, who called a group captain, who asked: 'What rank are you?' And when he heard I was a lowly pilot officer he said: 'You can go back by boat.' So I was driven off to the Hook of Holland by some bloke who whinged all the way about using up his petrol allowance.

I was left to my own devices until we got to Harwich, where I was met by somebody from Special Branch who whipped me through customs and put me on the train to London. I was standing on the platform at Liverpool Street station in my flying suit, with a life jacket on my shoulders, and a young cockney walked past me and said: 'Have you just bailed out, mate?' I said: 'Yes.' And he said, 'Bloody hard luck . . .' and walked on.

I had a ticket to West Malling, but by this time I was absolutely penniless, because they hadn't been very forthcoming at the Consulate, despite my losing all my money when I ditched. So I was setting off for a pretty long hike when the window in the signal box opened, and the stationmaster said: 'Are you the bloke who bailed out? Want a lift?' He even bought me a cup of tea, and then whipped me up to the squadron.

Everybody was in the bar when I got there and it was drinks all round, although not before I gave a fiver to the lad who had packed my parachute, which was a bit of a tradition in the squadron. The doctor sent me away on what they call survivors' leave for three weeks, so I went home to my parents in Cheshire. My mother was very upset. She'd been sent a telegram the day it all happened which said: 'Aircraft crashed into the sea', and thought she'd lost me, so I was treated royally as the long-lost son.

When I got back to my squadron, I was a bit out on a limb, because I didn't have a pilot, so I just flew with anybody who didn't have a navigator at the time. Eventually I found a pilot to crew up with me, and we flew together for the next two and a half years.

I don't really bring it to mind that much, well, I try not to, and I don't lose sleep over it any more, although once in a while I think: Here I am pushing eighty, and still alive ... Thank you, God.

RAY CRISFORD

There I was, on my tod, wondering what the hell was going to happen to me . . .

Well, I was born and bred in Eastbourne and was at school when the Battle of Britain was on, and saw all these planes tearing about all over the place. For the size of the town,

Eastbourne had more bombs dropped on it, so we had air raids pretty frequently, and as a youngster I thought, Cor, I would like to be part of that!

After leaving school I became a bank clerk at Barclays, although I had tried to volunteer when I was eighteen. But it turns out that my boss, who had been a lieutenant-colonel in the First World War, rang my father up – I didn't know this until afterwards – and said, 'This young whippersnapper wants to join the RAF, and he's too young to go off and get killed, can we keep him back?' So they both put pressure on me to delay joining up and I agreed, and didn't actually join until I was nineteen.

Although I had never even been in an aircraft I wanted to be a pilot, and I qualified for training and was sent to America on something called the Arnold Scheme, through which Churchill had done a deal with Roosevelt whereby the Yanks agreed to train goodness knows how many thousands of British pilots. I was Class 42E, which meant I would qualify in May 1942.

We left from Liverpool in a huge convoy of about thirty ships; I was on the *Highland Princess*, which was a banana boat from Brazil. We slept in the refrigeration area, and in order to be ready for an attack we weren't allowed to undress; the only thing we were allowed to remove at night was our boots, so we slept in hammocks with other people's feet practically in our face.

It was a hell of a trip, because the sea was absolutely appalling, and one night we were actually attacked. The day before, a Focke-Wulf had been circling, and we were warned that might lead to an attack, and, sure enough, that night we were attacked by a submarine; we heard depth charges, but in the morning the

Officer Commanding Troops said, 'You will be pleased to know we sank that submarine,' which was a great relief.

We landed at Halifax, Nova Scotia, and went by train to Toronto, where we stayed for about a week. The Canadians were absolutely wonderful. A lot of people came round and invited us to their homes. I remember one lady by the name of Mrs Thomas, who was a widow from the First World War: we went to her house and had a fabulous meal there – we had been on RAF rations beforehand, which were pretty meagre – and then she drove us back to the base.

We then went by train down to Albany in Georgia, which took about two days. To avoid contravening the Geneva Convention, we had to cross the border from Canada into America in civvies, as we were technically operating as civilians, and had been issued with grey suits.

The first six weeks of flying school we were in what they called Lower Class. As a Lower Classman, when you had a meal you had to eat at attention, and you were watched, and they made bloody sure you did it, and every lunchtime we had to march into the mess hall with a bugler, drums and the American flag.

Well, the Yanks taught us to fly by the seat of our pants. I learned on a Steerman, which was a biplane, a glorified Tiger Moth really, and had no instruments other than the gyroscope and an altimeter, so you could keep level. But they were lovely planes, wonderfully balanced; you could throttle back when you were in the air, put the nose up a bit and actually stall, and the thing would come down like a lift; it didn't go into a spin like any other aircraft.

The Yanks were so insular. They'd ask, 'Where are you from?' 'England.' 'Oh, where's that?' And that's no exaggeration. But they were incredibly friendly though. The same thing happened in Albany as in Toronto; they knew when our day finished, and you would walk down to the entrance to the airfield and there would be a row of about a dozen cars, everyone asking, 'Anyone want to come out for the evening?'

But also, we were in the deep South, where the blacks were third-class citizens. For instance, if you got on a bus the only seats the blacks were allowed to use were in the back rows, and if the bus was full they would be turfed off, which we found most embarrassing. I remember one night four of us went to the cinema in Albany, bought our tickets and sat up in the circle. When the lights went up, we were the only white people there. It turned out those seats were Blacks Only; whites were meant to sit in the stalls.

December the 7th 1943 was a Sunday, and we were all at Albany High School watching an American football game. During the interval, about thirty of our chaps played a demonstration English rugby match, and the crowd thought we were completely bonkers, because all we wore was a shirt, shorts and a pair of boots, whereas American footballers have helmets, shoulder pads, even pads on their legs. I mean, they look like men from Mars, don't they? Anyway, in the middle of all this, the Tannoy went: 'Attention please. Will all British cadets report back to the airfield at once!' And then about two seconds later: 'This is an order.' We all wondered what the hell was going on. When we got back, the Steermans were in a dead-straight line, and it turned out we had been brought back to disperse them, in case there was an air raid here in Albany. 'Air raid?' we said. 'Who's going to bomb us? Have you any idea how far Japan is from here?'

Anyway, our training continued, although we now ditched our civvies and put on our RAF uniforms. We then had to get used to flying the Hurricane, and we did mock combat manoeuvres in the air. The Hurricane was a lovely aircraft, great fun and exhilarating to fly; it wasn't as fast as the Spit, of course, but it could outturn a Spit in a tight turn.

Having finished our OTU training, we came back to England and I got a telegram to report to RAF Hunsdon, which was a wartime airfield with Nissen huts. I was lucky enough to join No. 3 Squadron, which was the Senior Fighter Squadron, dating back to May 1912, when they were the first squadron to get 'heavier than air machines'.

In early '43 we were one of the first squadrons to have the Hawker Typhoon, which was a brand new aircraft that had never really been tested. Typhoons were bastards to fly; they reckoned if you got into a spin in a Tiffy, that was it, you never got out. They were devils to land too, because there was only about eight or nine inches' clearance from prop to ground, so if you actually tried to land level, as you would in a Hurricane, you would plough in: in fact, a lot of chaps killed themselves landing. Taking off was fairly difficult too; you had to do it blind, because of the clearance of the prop, and it was only after you had levelled off that you could see the horizon.

Monday 13 September 1943, I had been on dawn cockpit readiness, and at about nine o'clock was released. But an hour later a lad came to the Nissen hut and said, 'Your squadron are needed, you're on ops.' There was reportedly a convoy coming down the Dutch coast, and we were sent off to attack it.

As we approached, the Jerries began firing tracer bullets like mad; I was coming in for the second pass, and was fairly low, twenty to thirty feet, something like that, and my engine was hit and started making a very rough noise, and I realised I had to get out.

The training meant you automatically knew what to do in an emergency. First of all, you got rid of your canopy: you pulled a lever and off it went. Then you undid your safety harness, brought your knees up, flipped the aircraft over and hoped you'd fall out. A lot of pilots were killed falling out, because they used to hit the tail plane, poor chaps. Anyway, I got out OK, pulled the ripcord and the parachute opened, and I thought, thank God for that, and literally, within a matter of seconds, I was in the water. I was knocked unconscious as I hit the sea, but I came to fairly quickly because the sea was pretty cold, and I just sat in my dinghy, and there I was, on my tod, wondering what the hell was going to happen to me.

As it happens, there was a fleet of Belgian fishing boats which actually saw me come down, and one boat came and picked me up. Unfortunately, of all the boats there was a Jerry in this one, armed as well, just in case they found people like me.

The Belgian lads were very good, actually; I was helped up on board, and stripped so they could dry my clothes out, and there was one lovely man, old enough to be my grandfather. He came up to me, passed me a piece of paper and a pencil, and, very quietly, whispered in broken English, 'Give me your address.' I put my parents' address on this piece of paper, and about four weeks later my parents received a telegram from the Air Ministry: 'Our friends on the Continent have advised us that your son is safe and well, and is a POW.'

I was taken to Zeebrugge, and handed over to the Jerries, and then I was put on an army lorry with an armed guard, driven to Brussels and shoved in jail. The Jerries kept saying, 'For you the war is over,' which I knew, but it still put the wind up me. I only spent one night in the Brussels jail, and was then sent to a camp near Frankfurt they had for RAF prisoners, and I spent the first eleven days in solitary confinement, being interviewed at odd times.

It was pretty scary being in solitary confinement, because you didn't know what the hell was going to happen to you. All you had in the room was a bunk with a straw mattress, and if you wanted to go to the toilet you banged on the door and, if you were lucky, a Jerry would come along and take you to the loo. Each day lasted one hell of a long time, because there was nothing to do except sit and wait for the next interrogation. The food was almost non-existent, the rations only just enough to keep you alive: mangel-wurzel soup, which was virtually just hot water, and two pieces of bread a day, and that was all.

They wanted to know who I was and where I was from, where I was stationed and what I was flying. Actually, I was flying from RAF Manston when I was shot down, but there was another Typhoon pilot, and he and I were put into a room with an interrogator. The Jerries thought we both came from Manston, because at that stage there weren't many Typhoon squadrons, but actually he was from another squadron. I had never seen him before in my life. Fortunately, we kept that from them, and I don't think we gave them any information that was of any help.

There were several hundred of us in this camp, in a fairly confined space. But there was one area, about forty, fifty yards long, where you could exercise. And that's where this chap, Richards, was. Squadron Leader Richards was in charge of the camp for the RAF, and he was chatting to everybody, this nice squadron leader in his uniform and cap and everything. I remember talking to him: 'Oh,' he said, 'how nice to meet you, glad you got here. No injuries? Tell me, what were you doing? What were you flying?' And naturally we talked to him, because he was a squadron leader, and you would open your heart, 'Well, I was flying Typhoons, 3 Squadron, from RAF Manston ...' but he was spying for the Jerries, the bastard. He was shot at the end of the war because he was an informer.

There wasn't much to do in this camp, but books came through from the British Red Cross and I did quite a bit of reading. Actually, I read a book about looking after chickens, and I thought, gosh, that sounds interesting and seriously thought that when I came home I was going to run a chicken farm. I also got involved in acting. We made a theatre set out of tea chests and God knows what else. There was one chap, Roy Dotrice, who in his pre-RAF days had been on the stage, and he organised play readings, which were great fun. The first play we put on was *Love from a Stranger*, which was based on an Agatha Christie short story, and we also did *She Stoops to Conquer*. I took part because I had done quite a bit of acting as a kid, and that occupied your mind because you had to learn your lines and do rehearsals.

And then one day we were all cleared from the camp, jammed

into cattle trucks and taken to Frankfurt. I can remember that first night very clearly, because it was possibly the scariest night of our lives for all of us. We had been put into marshalling yards with guards outside, and there was an air raid – the RAF were coming over in their hundreds – and all you heard were these bombs going off for hours. Fortunately, none dropped on us, but we would have been pretty good targets in the marshalling yards.

In the morning we continued on and ended up in a camp at Heidekrug in Lithuania, but then we moved out when the Russians were getting pretty near. I was one of the lucky ones, because I went by cattle truck down into Poland, and into an army camp, but the remainder, poor devils, were taken to Stettin and put on board a ship, where they were put in the hold, with no food or water, and a lot of them died.

The last camp I was at was Vollenbasse, but we were turfed out of there because the Jerries thought we were going to be over-run by the British and Americans, and were force-marched due east. We never slept under cover at night – we were always out in the open – and it was bitterly cold. We covered ourselves with leaves to try and keep warm, but it was impossible. One day the Jerries heard the Russians were coming, and of course the Jerries were dead scared of the Russians, so we about-turned, and marched westwards, and ended up on Lurembourg Heath, which is a great big open area like the Ashdown Forest in Sussex, but on a much bigger scale. We woke up one morning, and somebody said, 'Where are the goons?' And they had all disappeared.

The next thing we knew some British Army lads came in and said, 'We have captured the Heath, the Germans have disap-peared, and you are free.' Later, an Army officer came in and said,

'Which of you lads can drive vehicles?' I put my hand up, and he said, 'Right, jump in one of these.' And there was a whole long row of Jerry vehicles, with the Jerries actually on the side of the road, looking pretty abject. 'Help yourself,' he said. I jumped into this clapped-out German army vehicle, and we crossed the River Elbe on one of these floating pontoons, which wasn't much wider than the vehicle. I can remember sweating blood driving that thing. We were there for about a day, and then we were picked up by Lancasters and flown home.

We landed at Dunsfold in Surrey, and the RAF had organised it marvellously: every single bloke who got off the aircraft was greeted by a wonderfully attractive WAAF, who also hugged us. I still feel very emotional about that; to this day it still makes me weep to remember it.

When I came home at the end of the war I weighed just eight stone, and had a big, distended stomach, although I found it very difficult to eat proper meals because my stomach had actually shrunk so much I couldn't take it, and I spent a lot of time in bed because I wasn't fit enough to be up. I was a bit of a mess, really. Although they hadn't yet identified it, I suppose I was suffering, like a lot of the others, from post-traumatic stress disorder. When I went back to the bank, I couldn't add up, I just couldn't get my brain working, and the staff had no sympathy for me. They all thought I was plain lazy, they had no idea what I was going through, because there were no visible signs that I was suffering.

It took a long time to get back to normality. I couldn't talk about the war for years; it was only in the last few years I have been able to talk about it. Funnily enough, when things are so long ago, you only remember the enjoyable bits, and I mostly loved my time in the RAF. All in all, I'm glad I had these wartime experiences; it was an adventure really. Also, it was nice to have been a small part of putting paid to Hitler.

Occasionally, I dream about being a POW and the various things that happened, and I wake up in a sweat. But I am grateful for being alive, quite honestly. I have been to six funerals this year already, two of which were Air Force chaps. Next June I shall be ninety, and the family have already decided what's going to happen, they're planning a big party. I just hope I get there. I'm under the doctor at the moment, I'm on Warfarin because I am suffering from low blood pressure, and, also, I am not terribly mobile because I have a bad back. But the best thing about my life is that I have got a wonderful family, who are wonderfully supportive; I've got three children, nine grandchildren and four great-grandchildren.

Danny Danziger has written sixteen books on a range of subjects including *We Are Soldiers* and *The Year 1000*, which went to number one and stayed on the bestseller list for seven months. Danny's weekly interview column 'Best of Times, Worst of Times' won many accolades and awards over twelve years.